AF614891

PRAISE FOR

HOW TO CLOSE A CAMP

"*How to Close a Camp* is critical reading for anyone trying to understand one of the defining cruelties of our time: the mass immigration detention centers that have sprung up across the country. Washington writes with clarity and urgency. His book is a moral manual, a rigorously researched guide to help readers fight back against this spreading evil." —**GREG GRANDIN**, author of *America, América: A New History of the New World*

"This is an urgent, courageous book. It is not just a comprehensive history of immigration detention camps as sites of social control and repression; it is also a compelling catalog of the many creative ways in which people have refused to be contained. Please read it, both to witness the vital stories that Washington captures with grace and rigor and to study the moral blueprint it presents to us all, to help us account for and shape the kind of world in which we hope to live. What could be more needed than that?" —**SARAH STILLMAN**, staff writer at *The New Yorker*

"*How to Close a Camp* showcases Washington's rich talent for weaving together the deep veins of anti-immigrant policy in the United States with a cogent analysis of the system and powerful, instructive stories of resistance. As immigrant detention becomes a testing ground for authoritarian rule, this book is a crucial resource for seasoned activists and those new to the issue alike." —**SILKY SHAH**, author of *Unbuild Walls: Why Immigrant Justice Needs Abolition*

"John Washington has written an important and timely book: a thorough reckoning of ICE through a deep historical analysis of this long-standing yet somewhat-unknown machine of terror, most starkly symbolized by its incarceration camps. Just as important, this book also vividly reports on the spirit of sustained and creative resistance that is needed to bring these camps down. A must-read." —**TODD MILLER**, author of *Build Bridges, Not Walls: A Journey to a World Without Borders*

"Immigration prisons are a profitable spectacle of violence. Through a careful blend of on-the-ground reporting and thoughtful analysis, journalist John Washington traces the roots of policymakers' choice to lock up migrants and brings to life the need—and possibility—of ending this type of human bondage." —**CÉSAR CUAUHTÉMOC GARCÍA HERNÁNDEZ**, author of *Welcome the Wretched: In Defense of the "Criminal Alien"*

"John Washington has written a timely, passionate call to action against mass detention and mass deportation. It is as much an inspiring battle plan as it is a searing indictment of the racism- and profit-driven deportation state. *How to Close a Camp* is a demand that something must be done and also offers proof that we can do a helluva lot. A must-read for our times." —**MICHAEL KAGAN**, author of *The Battle to Stay in America: Immigration's Hidden Front Line*

HOW TO CLOSE A CAMP

DISPATCHES FROM THE FIGHT AGAINST IMMIGRANT DETENTION

JOHN WASHINGTON

HAYMARKET BOOKS
CHICAGO, ILLINOIS

© 2026 John Washington

Published in 2026 by
Haymarket Books
P.O. Box 180165
Chicago, IL 60618
773-583-7884
www.haymarketbooks.org
info@haymarketbooks.org

ISBN: 979-888890-816-7

Distributed to the trade in the US through Consortium Book Sales and Distribution (www.cbsd.com) and internationally through Ingram Publisher Services International (www.ingramcontent.com).

This book was published with the generous support of Lannan Foundation, Wallace Action Fund, and the Marguerite Casey Foundation.

Special discounts are available for bulk purchases by organizations and institutions. Please email info@haymarketbooks.org for more information.

Cover design by Rachel Cohen.

Printed in Canada by union labor.

Library of Congress Cataloging-in-Publication data is available.
Library of Congress Control Number: 2026941409

10 9 8 7 6 5 4 3 2 1

For D and E

was the sugar so sweet
you forgot the sugarcane?
—**Anne Yukie Watanabe**, "instructions to, 1942,"
collected in *The Gate of Memory: Poems by
Descendants of Nikkei Wartime Incarceration*

Abolitionists were original and critical
thinkers on democracy, not simply romantic
reformers who confined themselves to
appeals to the heart.
—**Manisha Sinha**, *The Slave's Cause*

CONTENTS

INTRODUCTION

Barrack-style white tents shelter hurricane-fence cages lined with bunks. Outside, rows of RVs and bathroom trailers sit next to a strip of shadeless pavement and stacks of generators. Three thousand people, stranded in the hot tents amid the buzzing sludge of a swamp, cut off from families, medical care, and lawyers: a spectacle of bondage masquerading as border security.

"Alligator Alcatraz," as the South Florida detention center has been dubbed, was built in eight days in the Everglades. The immigration camp was constructed in the first heady months of the second Trump administration's assault on immigrants and, at least briefly, was the centerpiece of the modern camp system in the United States, reminding migrants that the very landscape of America can be weaponized against them.

"We're going to teach them how to run away from an alligator if they escape prison," Trump gloated shortly after the camp opened.[1] The first state-owned and -operated immigration detention facility in the United States, the camp has no federal oversight, and it is not integrated into the systems or databases of Immigration and Customs Enforcement (ICE). Those locked up are thus left mostly incommunicado to the outside.

In 2025 the camp quickly swallowed around $360 million in state construction contracts and is projected to require approximately $450 million for its first year of operation.

Funds for construction came primarily from the Florida Division of Emergency Management, under emergency procurement powers typically reserved for natural disasters, and the Federal Emergency Management Agency approved $608 million in reimbursement funding.[2] (In the last forty-five years, there have been ninety-four natural disasters in the state with losses exceeding $1 billion dollars each.)[3]

Just months after the camp opened, people locked inside revolted. Guards responded with tear gas and beatings. People outside revolted, too: Environmental groups and members of the Miccosukee Nation filed a lawsuit claiming the facility trampled on both human rights and the already enfragiled ecosystem. The Miccosukee began living in that strip in the Everglades after escaping the nineteenth-century campaign of extermination and forced removal to reservations—among the earliest iterations of the camp—to hide out deep in the swamplands. After the Miccosukee and others pushed back against the South Florida detention facility, a federal judge ordered the camp to be shut down.

As the administration begrudgingly complied, hundreds of the migrants held there went missing—lost somewhere in the opaque labyrinth of the camp system, some probably already deported.[4] Less than a month after the judicial order to close the camp was issued, the Eleventh Circuit Court reversed course and the facility was reopened. Meanwhile, reports of the conditions inside described people held in cages for days at a time, lights on 24/7, power outages prompting extreme temperatures, swarms of mosquitoes, poor and insufficient food, broken telephones making it impossible to reach attorneys, and people constantly shackled when they briefly left the pens. According to one legal complaint, "Food portions are extremely small, sometimes full of maggots, and detainees suffer from frequent hunger."[5] Reports describe a punishment "box," a two-by-two-foot outdoor cage into which people are crammed and exposed to the elements for up to twenty-four hours. According to Amnesty International, when people are put in the box, "their hands are shackled and their feet are attached to restraints on the ground. They are unable to sit down or move positions, and are forced to remain there for hours in the heat with hardly any water or protection from the sun, heat and insects." One asylum seeker told researchers, "People ended up in the 'box' just for asking the guards for anything. I saw a guy who was put in it for an entire day."[6]

The administration is announcing other branded camps—all bearing their sophomoric alliterative bent: the Louisiana Lockup, the Speedway Slammer, the Cornhusker Clink. The names matter. They represent a return: away from an obsessive focus on the border and the spectacle of the wall, and back to interior enforcement. The message is that no place, and nobody—newcomer or citizen, adult or child—is safe. Tom Homan, Trump's "border czar," made that message clear in 2024 shortly before the Trump administration returned to office. "You better be looking over your shoulder," he told migrants.[7] The sinister specter of the camp is central to that threat, a signal of just how far the state is willing to go. Abracadabra, Midway Blitz, Red Card, Zulu Shield, Tidal Wave. All real names for real ICE operations: heavily armed masked agents fanning out through US cities, warring against civilians, filling the camps.

What is a camp? What are these tools of containment and torture, these embodiments of fear and banners of nationalist violence? A camp—which in this book will largely refer to prisons or jails built or operated to lock up migrants—is society seeing certain groups of people as unwanted and disposable. A camp is distraction from entrenched political failure—scapegoating "the other" for societal deterioration, underfunded public education and declining literacy, expensive and inconsistently available healthcare, and ethical anomie. A camp is a refusal to take responsibility for or reckon with the cataclysm of climate change, war, economic terrorism, and the normalization of pervasive neglect, disregard of the rule of law, and chasmic and ever-widening inequalities. A camp is a society turning its back on a basic sense of morality.

A CAMP IS A MAN WHO NEVER TASTES FRESH FRUIT AND BARELY SEES THE SUN FOR FIVE YEARS.[8]

A CAMP IS A 16-MONTH-OLD BABY LOSING A THIRD OF HIS BODY WEIGHT FROM DIARRHEA, AND HIS MOTHER, BEGGING CAMP DOCTORS FOR HELP, SENT AWAY WITH PEDIALYTE.[9]

A CAMP IS A MAN WITH EPILEPSY SENT TO SOLITARY CONFINEMENT AS PUNISHMENT FOR REQUESTING HIS MEDICATION, THEN DYING ALONE IN A CELL FROM A SEIZURE.[10]

A CAMP IS A VENEZUELAN HAIRDRESSER KIDNAPPED BY ICE AND RENDERED TO EL SALVADOR, WHERE HE IS SENT TO THE TERRORISM CONFINEMENT CENTER, HAS HIS HEAD SHAVED BY MASKED MEN, IS BEATEN, RAPED, AND REPEATEDLY TOLD, "YOU'LL NEVER LEAVE THIS PLACE ALIVE."[11]

A camp is close to where you live, work, organize. Camps are nearly everywhere, with hundreds of "detention centers," "processing centers," "holding facilities," as well as leased local jail and prison cells in every state of America and in many countries throughout the world. We are building more of them and locking away more people. A camp warps and degrades reality both for those in fear of ending up in one and for those living alongside them. Our decisions as a society, meanwhile, are uprooting more and more people from their homes, pushing people to flee, and failing to meet them with the protection, basic rights, freedom, or dignity they seek. The question we must ask about closing the camp is not *if* or *why* or *when*, but only *how*.

But to be able to close a camp, we must understand what a camp is. We must look at campaigns to close or block camps since the first of them—the reservations, the ships, the "Chinese jails" and Ellis and Angel Islands—opened and understand what those fights accomplished and how. More than a century of resistance, refusal, and grassroots activism has taught us that we need to pry into the legal, practical, and political mechanisms of how camps are built and function. At the same time, we will never permanently close the camps until we learn how to build something different and more humane—not cages—in their place.

The proliferation of the camp is very likely to accelerate. We have seen the camp expanded and redeployed in the past to target not just migrants but also racialized groups and so-called political subversives. During the internment period in the 1940s, the US built and operated ten large concentration camps. As historian Brianna Nofil explains, once the infrastructure is built out, it is utilized, and targeted populations can shift and expand. "When the INS [Immigration and Naturalization

Service] moved noncitizens to internment camps, it placed them on the same deportation trains, supervised by the same deportation officers who had expelled thousands of migrants from the United States in the prior two decades," Nofil writes.[12] The mechanism of the camp can be universally deployed. As a tool, it can manacle any neck—native or newcomer.

In the 1950s, the US government reframed immigration as a national security threat, seeing migrants and others as political enemies. Much like Palestinian activist Mahmoud Khalil was targeted in 2025, in 1950 Congress enacted, over Harry Truman's veto, the McCarran Internal Security Act, which established the Subversive Activities Control Board and enabled the "emergency detention" of anyone (US citizens included) who committed "espionage or sabotage."

"Mass incarceration is mass elimination," writes historian Kelly Lytle Hernández in *City of Inmates: Conquest, Rebellion, and the Rise of Human Caging in Los Angeles, 1771–1965*. "Incarceration operates as a means of purging, removing, caging, containing, erasing, disappearing, and eliminating targeted populations from land, life, and society in the United States."[13] That is the logic of the camp: fear, hate, punishment, torture, banishment, death.

Stakes are high. The status quo is frightening, and the near future is likely significantly worse. But pessimism, as the saying goes, is a luxury we can't afford.

"I know that what I am asking is impossible," James Baldwin wrote in 1963. "But in our time, as in every time, the impossible is the least that one can demand."[14] The demand is to close the camp.

Where We're At

On January 20, 2025, the first day of his second term, Trump issued an executive order, Protecting the American People Against Invasion, instructing the secretary of homeland security to "promptly take all appropriate action and allocate all legally available resources or establish contracts to construct, operate, control, or use facilities to detain removable aliens. The Secretary of Homeland Security, further, shall take all appropriate actions to ensure the detention of aliens apprehended for violations of immigration law."[15]

In April, ICE cited an "unusual and compelling urgency" to rush no-bid contracts for more camps, and soon they would have the money to dish out.[16]

In July, Trump signed the 2025 Reconciliation Bill, the so-called One Big Beautiful Bill, allocating more than $170 billion over four years for border and interior enforcement, with a stated goal of deporting one million immigrants a year—roughly three times the previous record for formal deportations (as opposed to quicker "turnbacks," or almost-immediate expulsions right at the border). That's more than the yearly budget for all the country's local and state law enforcement agencies combined. It gives ICE a bigger budget than all but fifteen of the world's militaries.[17] It was also more than a threefold increase to ICE's already-bloated budget, giving them $75 billion over four years, or about $18.7 billion annually. Added to the $10 billion Congress had already appropriated for ICE for fiscal year 2025, the agency suddenly had $28.7 billion to wreak havoc with. That's $23 billion more than the agency was allocated in 2010.

Besides heaping money into detention, in 2025 ICE's spending on small arms and ordnance, compared to 2024 levels, skyrocketed by 700 percent.[18] The agency also earmarked $200 million for an ad campaign, including dishing multimillion-dollar contracts directly to friends of Kristi Noem, then the secretary of the Department of Homeland Security (DHS).[19] The campaign resulted in overproduced videos posted on X that made American cities look like dystopian *Doom* landscapes, *Star Wars* memes with overmuscled AI portraits of Trump, and beachside 1960s-styled visions of what a white America could look like after one hundred million deportations: "The peace of a nation no longer besieged by the third world."[20]

But Trump's budget did more than pour billions into cages, guns, and white supremacist fantasies; it further encoded cruelty into the architecture of US immigration policy. Two-thirds of that funding—$45 billion over four years—will be used for camps, locking up potentially more than 100,000 people per year. The $11.25 billion added to ICE's annual detention budget makes for a 400 percent increase from the previous year.[21] It surpasses the 2026 Department of Justice budget request for the federal prison system, which holds 155,000 people. By early 2026, ICE laid out plans to spend over $38 billion on new and expanded detention camps.[22] The 2025 budget bill also allows ICE to build more camps to jail families, usually mothers with their children, and—in clear contravention of a decades-old settlement limiting the detention of children to twenty days—removes limits on how long they can be detained. In the first ten months of 2025, about 600 children who had been living in the US were picked up by ICE and put in government-run shelters—with significantly more young children captured, along with their families, at or after crossing the border—and locked into camps.[23] In the first seven months of Trump's second term, immigration authorities arrested the parents of at least 11,000 US citizen children —an average of 50 a day.[24] In October, CNN reported that DHS was planning to funnel as much as $10 billion from the US Navy to build camps with capacities of 10,000 people.[25] By early 2026, DHS was paying tens of millions of dollars to buy Amazon-style warehouses near deportation airport hubs to detain migrants in what one official called "mega detention centers."[26]

In September, the Board of Immigration Appeals (unlike other courts, the BIA is part of the executive branch, thus ultimately controlled by the president) ruled that no undocumented migrants who entered the country without inspection would be eligible for release on bond. So-called discretionary releases dropped by 87 percent.[27] In other words, the camp became mandatory: indefinite detention without the benefit of due process or trial by jury. In May 2025, White House deputy chief of staff and longtime anti-immigrant zealot Stephen Miller said that the Trump administration was "actively looking at" suspending habeas corpus, one of the bedrock legal principles of modern democracies, first articulated more than eight hundred years ago in the Magna Carta.[28] *Habeas corpus*, Latin for "produce the body," protects a person from illegal or arbitrary detention.*

* In 1933, Adolf Hitler convinced German President Paul von Hindenburg to suspend habeas corpus as part of the Reichstag Fire Decree, paving the way for the first Nazi concentration camps. Let us not forget: Revisiting history in order to take precautionary measures is practicing prudence, not alarmism.

In June 2025, ICE issued a "hold room" waiver, extending the maximum time people could be held in facilities supposed to be used only for temporary detention. Previously, one could only be locked up in these small holding rooms for twelve hours; the waiver extended that to seventy-two hours, trapping people in cold, lights-constantly-beaming, bare-bones cages without access to medical care or attorneys for three days. Amnesty International found people were stuffed into these small, freezing-cold facilities, weren't fed, and weren't given access to toilets or showers for even longer.[29]

The result of indiscriminate detention—combined with the unleashing of ICE, Border Patrol, and the US military on American streets—is a state of despotism, suffering, and death. The number of "at-large" arrests—arrests conducted in communities—rose by 600 percent, and the number of people arrested who had no criminal record rose by 2,450 percent.[30] Prior ICE guidance to limit agents from tracking people down and arresting them at schools, hospitals, and places of worship was revoked. For anyone who still thought citizenship conferred protection from the onslaught, the first nine months of the Trump administration poured cold water on that misconception. *ProPublica* counted nearly two hundred US citizens arrested, including at least twenty children, two of whom had cancer.[31] In one case, four US citizen children were held for twenty days in a cement-floor ten-by-ten cell with nothing but thin mats to lie on and a toilet in the corner.[32] In Minneapolis, immigration officers identified and tracked down citizens at their homes.[33] In the first weeks of 2026, immigration officers also assassinated two US citizens, Renee Good and Alex Pretti, for getting in their way.

At the same time, what methods of accountability exist, meager as they are, are being dismantled. Members of Congress, despite express legal authority permitting their access, are increasingly barred from entering detention camps. Offices tasked with monitoring civil rights abuses have been shuttered or gutted. Fees for asylum and other humanitarian protections have been jacked up to levels most people cannot pay. What emerges is not just a system of detention but one of attrition and exclusion—designed to enrich contractors, incite fear, stoke nationalist fervor, and sever immigrants from the thinnest remaining threads of due process. The deaths mounting inside detention—triple the pace of previous years, *at least*—are not aberrations but auguries. They testify to what happens when a democracy convinces itself that some lives are so worthless they can be hidden away, warehoused, banished.

And ICE, ever eager for more personnel, began offering a $50,000 sign-on bonus for new recruits. Reporting in early 2026 showed that ICE was spending $100 million in a "wartime recruitment" effort, lowering their hiring standards, deploying overtly white supremacist tropes in their hiring ads and, according to one DHS official speaking anonymously, signing on people who can "barely read or write."[34] Training time for the recruits was cut by two-thirds. In an adulatory, dear-leader-like move, the new training period was set to forty-seven days—a direct nod to Trump, the forty-seventh president.[35] As one observer put it, "We're launching manhunts with $50,000 bonuses for misdemeanors and civil infractions," holding people "without due process in conditions that kill them."[36]

Amid the intentional cruelty, puerile symbolism, and rapid camp expansion, private prison firms are circling the halls of power. Months before Trump signed the bill to dedicate an unprecedented amount of money to detention, ICE set up an expedited contract process and was already soliciting bids from for-profit prison corporations.[37] The two largest companies, CoreCivic and GEO Group, longtime financial supporters of the president, have both frequently wooed former high-level ICE officials into their ranks.[38] To illustrate the rapidly revolving door between ICE and the private sector—or the camp as cash machine—consider Daniel A. Bible, who worked as ICE's top official in charge of immigration detention until he was hired by GEO Group days before the 2024 presidential election. That same year, while GEO Group donated $1 million to Trump-aligned political action committees, according to an article from the Project on Government Oversight (POGO), ICE committed $747.4 million in contracts to the company—a pretty damn good return on investment.[39] In an earnings call held just days after Trump won the election, and with Bible already on the payroll, GEO Group predicted a $400 million boost in company revenue.

Current border czar Tom Homan—frequently the White House's mouthpiece defending the anti-immigrant rampage—has also previously contracted with GEO Group. In 2025, FBI agents caught Homan taking a cash bribe of $50,000 to help business execs looking to land contracts with the federal government.[40] (While Homan never denied taking the money, Trump's Justice Department closed an investigation into the matter.)

In May, the CEO of CoreCivic told investors, "Never in our 42-year company history have we had so much activity and demand for our services as we are seeing right now."[41] "The system hasn't malfunctioned," as César Cuauhtémoc García Hernández writes in *Migrating to Prison*. "It was intended to punish, stigmatize, and marginalize—all for political and financial gain."[42]

■■■

As I write these words, reports break that ICE plans to expand its total camp capacity in the US to 108,000 beds.[43] As you read these words, that number may have already been reached, or surpassed, or perhaps pushback and shutdown campaigns have slowed or even reversed the expansion. None of it is enough. Until we, as a society, reject the camp and its logic, the camp will remain a threat. And not only a threat, but the linchpin in the entire immigration enforcement regime. In early November 2025, when asked about federal agents tackling unarmed mothers to the ground, using tear gas on protesters, and smashing car windows, Trump said such tactics "haven't gone far enough."[44] This is a prime example, as scholar Michelle Castañeda writes in *Disappearing Rooms: The Hidden Theaters of Immigration Law*, of "force compensating for fragility."[45] Despite Stephen Miller's claim that "we will prevail over the forces of wickedness and evil," coalitions built on fear and hate never last.[46] They are always fragile, always vulnerable.

Why *Camp*?

An immigration detention camp is not the same as a prisoner of war camp, a refugee or displaced person camp, a forced labor camp, a concentration camp, or an extermination camp.*

* The nomenclature of camps is vast and also includes assembly centers (an early name for internment camps in the US), filtration camps (camps for prisoners of war exchanged between the Third

Within each of these categories, levels of confinement, savagery, lawlessness, and dehumanization vary. Yet they are of the same genus, and it is revealing to articulate the similarities between them, and what distinguishes a camp from a prison, or camp life from noncamp life (even when that includes ghettoes, slums, favelas, or other structural conditions of precarization and expropriation, including general attacks on ways and qualities of life that can generate camplike conditions).

While it's important not to elide historical variance, the word *camp* maintains shades of its superlative forms—concentration or extermination camps—and those shades are germane, and why I believe *camp* is most apt for immigration detention. Italian philosopher Giorgio Agamben calls the variations of camp a "progression," suggesting that there is slippage among them, that it isn't so hard to cross the line from a camp that confines people to one that hastens social or legal death—and ultimately to one that exterminates. Agamben writes: "Internment camps, concentration camps, extermination camps represent a perfectly real filiation."[47]

A definitional aspect of camps—all camps—is that they strip people of, or at least diminish, their legal personhood. And while people held in immigration camps are not

---

Reich and the Soviet Union during World War II), and silence camps (*Schweigelager*, the Nazi concentration camps taken over by the Soviets after the war). Scholar Elliott Young makes a case for some US mental asylums to be considered camps, especially as disproportionate numbers of migrants were confined to them in the early twentieth century. See Young, *Forever Prisoners: How the United States Made the World's Largest Immigrant Detention System* (New York: Oxford University Press, 2021).

completely outside the sphere of law, they are, as we will see, mocked by the law. Given immigration courts' clear kangaroo characteristics—including mass trials and the fact that both judge and prosecutor work for the same boss, the executive branch—it is a stretch to say that immigrants are afforded any semblance of justice. As Dan Stone, author of *A Very Short Introduction to Concentration Camps*, writes of people held in immigration camps, "They are very close to falling into [philosopher Hannah] Arendt's category of the superfluous stateless person from whom the 'right to have rights' has been removed."[48]

The immigration camp, as I define it, is the carceral confinement and control of people deemed unwanted or "out of place." A society might designate an individual or community as unwanted to maintain a racial order, exploit surplus labor, neutralize a perceived political threat, or try to distract from societal ills. They do so by targeting, marginalizing, and scapegoating those individuals or communities. And while that targeting is typically focused on migrants—as we're using the term here—it's important to avoid overreliance on or simplification of that designation: nonmigrants, including citizens, are also interrogated by immigration agents and sometimes arrested and held in camps to be deported.*

---

* The terms *migrant*, *immigrant*, *undocumented alien*, and other variants can't fully capture the context of forced displacement, violently imposed and shifting borders, and the stripping of legal status. I've chosen to mostly use *migrant* in this book because, I believe, it captures both a variety of reasons people move as well as their agency; it's also a term I find many people, those forced to or choosing to move across borders, use themselves.

While immigration camps also share similarities with prisons and jails, they are categorically different. People held in camps are being confined (in effect, punished) not for something they allegedly did but because of *who or where they are.* This constitutes an even more penetrating attack on their personhood.

Deep within its very definition, a camp carries a dangerous, manufactured distinction between people. The existence of the camp is an a priori conception that some people belong and others do not, that some people have rightful claims to territory or rights and others do not. In other words, and importantly, the idea of the camp extends beyond its physical structure. People don't have to be confined within the walls of the camp to be consigned to the camp's violence, logic, and reach.

While the word *camp* in this context most obviously calls to mind the concentration camps that killed millions in the Holocaust, we can look to US history for two blueprints for the modern immigration camp: the Indian reservations and the Japanese American internment camps. Historian Kathleen DuVal, in *Native Nations*, writes that the 1830 Indian Removal Act resulted in "one of the country's most extreme violations of sovereignty and human rights, [when] it ultimately expelled tens of thousands of people from their homes and crowded them into Indian Territory."[49] While the move was based in nineteenth-century law, its motivations had roots in the nation's founding. Thomas Jefferson, for example, insisted in 1780 that the Shawnee people move west or be wiped out because "the same world will scarcely do for them and us."[50] Jefferson's quip captures a fundamental logic of the camp: an unwillingness to share space. Both the reservation system and, later, Indian boarding schools were designed to restrict mobility, to detain (or encamp), and obliterate difference through violence—setting a precedent still followed today in cultural, political, legal, and physical attacks against immigrants. "You are not allowed to be here" is only a few steps away—and sometimes no steps away—from "You are not allowed to be." That is the continuum we reject when we reject the camp.

Even before the United States was founded, Spanish colonizers in the Southwest in the 1600s implemented the strategy of *reducción* to try to corral and immobilize Native populations. As DuVal explains, the Spanish "aimed to 'reduce' Native people from what they saw as their barbarous nomadic way of life into the concentrated and permanent towns like those of Spain."[51] The *reducción* (and later the reservation system), the border wall, and immigration detention are variations on a single architecture.

The paradigm of the nation-state presupposes an excluded other: groups (to varying extents) persecuted and thrust out from under the protection of the law. The exclusion, hounding, and locking away of populations is not a symptom of a country protecting itself from an outsider or threat, or a sequela of internal safekeeping, but an inherent part of what makes a nation-state. The process is the fictional creation of what scholar Mahmood Mamdani calls "permanent minorities"—populations stripped of rights and immobilized.[52] Agamben calls the camp "the fundamental biopolitical paradigm of the West."[53] Secretary of State Marco Rubio said as much at the Munich Security Conference in February 2026: "We are part of one civilization—Western civilization," he intoned, explaining why the Trump administration is so desperate to slam the nation's doors and clean house of the people they don't want.[54] The West defines itself ("centuries of shared history, Christian faith, culture, heritage, language, ancestry," in Rubio's words) such that the camp is necessary to maintain borders both around the edges and within the national artifice. In other words, the camp is one of the ultimate expressions of the nation-state.

Of the Nazi concentration camps, French philosopher Maurice Blanchot wrote, "Know what has happened, do not forget, and at the same time never will you know."[55] He argues that we can never fully capture or understand the horrors experienced in the Third Reich's death camps, or in the camps feeding the Khmer Rouge's "killing fields." One difference between those camps and the immigration camps of today is that now, *we do know*. People caged inside them, advocates and allies working to support them, and journalists reporting on them have told us, again and again, what the camps are.

Polish sociologist Zygmunt Bauman called the twentieth century "the century of camps."[56] Only a quarter of the way through the twenty-first century, let these hundred years not be a repeat, or worse.

Camp Anywhere

Modern US immigration camps can take many forms. They can be privately run detention centers, federally owned service-processing centers, "short term" Border Patrol holding facilities, massive clusters of tents on military bases, or cells in local jails.* They are occasionally

* In the days of American chattel slavery, human holding pens were known as barracoons, related to the term *barrack*.

hotel rooms. Camps also include so-called alternatives to detention: Nearly four hundred thousand migrants in the US, at a peak in 2022, were shackled with electronic monitoring devices or under other forms of "supervision" and surveillance.[57]

We also need to look beyond borders—an implicit refrain of this book—to the international outsourcing of camps. By 2025, the United States relied on a global constellation of camps to lock up migrants, including at its naval base at Guantánamo, a shipping container on a military base in Djibouti, a gulag in El Salvador, a "migrant care" center in Costa Rica, and a hotel in Panama.* In the

* On any given day, hundreds of thousands of people across the world are held in camps merely because of their immigration status. According to the Global Detention Project, countries currently imprisoning migrants include Afghanistan, Albania, Antigua and Barbuda, Armenia, Australia, Austria, Azerbaijan, The Bahamas, Bahrain, Bangladesh, Belgium, Bosnia and Herzegovina, Botswana, Bulgaria, Cambodia, Canada, Chile, Costa Rica, Croatia, Curaçao, Cyprus, Czech Republic, Denmark, Dominica, Dominican Republic, Egypt, El Salvador, Estonia, Finland, France, Gabon, Germany, Greece, Guatemala, Honduras, Hong Kong, India, Ireland, Israel, Italy, Japan, Jordan, Kosovo, Kuwait, Kyrgyzstan, Latvia, Lebanon, Liechtenstein, Libya, Luxembourg, Malaysia, Maldives, Malta, Mauritania, Mexico, Moldova, Morocco, Nicaragua, Niger, The Netherlands, Oman, Panama, The Philippines, Poland, Portugal, Qatar, Romania, Russia, Saudi Arabia, Serbia, Singapore, Slovenia, South Africa, South Korea, Spain, Sri Lanka, Sweden, Switzerland, Taiwan, Thailand, Trinidad and Tobago, Tunisia, Turkey, Ukraine, United Arab Emirates, United Kingdom, Vietnam, Yemen, and Zimbabwe.

summer of 2025, the Trump administration rendered eight men to South Sudan and five men to the small African nation of Eswatini, formerly known as Swaziland. None of the five sent to Eswatini had ever been there before, and they weren't told where they were being sent, by military transport plane, until minutes before they touched down. They were later incarcerated in a maximum-security prison. One of the men, 62-year-old Orville Etoria from Jamaica, told *The New Yorker* the trip brought to mind the Middle Passage: "To be honest, it helped me imagine how the slaves might have felt, going to another land in shackles and chains—that loneliness, that disconnect, that sense of loss."[58]

■■■

Always alive has been the resistance. For as long as the camp and its attending massacres and ethnic cleansings have been wielded, they have been met with rejection. People have pushed back: walked away, cried foul—refused to be contained.

Across half a millennium, the struggle has never only been about land—who has the right to claim, control, protect, live on, or exploit it—but also about movement: the right to remain and the right to leave. After all, the first instinct of conquest is to dictate movement—forcing some to scatter, others to stay penned in. A detention cage and the threat of deportation is the most absolute form of controlling motion, the distillation of colonizing logic. The body is fixed, the horizon narrowed, and the possibility of movement foreclosed.

Yet even in the darkest hours, lines have been walked, rivers crossed, boundaries not militarized but celebrated. Historian and ethnobotanist Gary Paul Nabhan, in *Against the American Grain: A Borderlands History of Resistance*, writes of the Yaqui resistance to the first Spanish colonizers' incursions into their native lands in modern-day Arizona and Sonora: to safeguard their territory, Yaqui elders and warriors took the approach of "singing the boundary" of their homelands.[59] They stood guard, shot poisoned arrows, danced, and repelled an invading army of slavers. They pushed back and kept the Spanish away for over seventy years, and they have never ceded their territory. Against the machinery of confinement, there persists the slow, stubborn knowledge that both movement and life itself are freedom, and that to protect them—whether with sail or song—is to resist the walls closing in.

In contemporary philosopher Thomas Nail's *Theory of the Border*, the border is not a line but a machine—an ever-moving apparatus that sorts, slows, and accelerates bodies according to the needs of power.[60] The walls are not simply built and then left to stand; they churn, adapt, and extend their reach deep into the interior of a nation and far beyond the frontier. The camp is one of the wall's purest expressions, a place where motion is not just halted but transformed into a slow attrition of life. To resist such a machine requires more than opposition at its edge; it demands a reimagining of movement itself as a collective, shared right—one that neither the state nor the border can legitimately grant or deny. In this sense, every march, caravan, legal fight, online campaign, or pot-and-pan rally is not only an act of refusal but a reclaiming of the world as a space meant to be shared and traversed.

■■■

The first and crucial step to closing a camp is being against the camp.

Not *a* camp, not *that* camp, not a newly proposed camp or this particularly atrocious camp. But against camp as concept, against camp as practice—against all camps. Against locking people up because of where they were born or where they are.

More practically—and also key to closing a camp—is the understanding that immigration detention camps are not abstract federal machines. They are, rather, deeply embedded in local political economies: counties that sign contracts with ICE, private prison companies that seek zoning permits and tax breaks, local health departments that license medical providers, and municipal governments that issue permits for food services and utility hookups. Every one of these nodes is a potential pressure point.

Camps can't be built and can't be run without the land sales, the staffing, or the licensing, permitting, and accreditation that legitimize them. They can't be built without enough people saying okay, turning their heads, remaining insulated from the horrors of the camp. Camps depend on the political will to build and maintain them. At the same time, they are susceptible to the will to shutter and repurpose them. A camp is a long series of choices that need frequent reaffirmation.

We can make different choices.

The Political Horizon

Along with establishing a posture of everyday resistance to the camp, another key to closing them is harnessing the legal system: writing and passing laws to decriminalize migration and to open borders. While such a legislative battle and ideological shift may seem uphill or beyond reach, the boundaries of this assumption were tested in 2018 as activists and lawmakers succeeded in drawing on widespread popular sentiment to popularize the slogan #AbolishIce. While the "campaign" proved short-lived and was enabled more by political expedience than principle, it proved that radical rhetorical shifts in the public's views on immigration are possible. During the 2020 presidential campaign, nine out of ten Democratic candidates raised their hands during a debate signaling they were in favor of decriminalizing unauthorized border crossings. That moment has been remembered less for its potential than as a political faceplant, as illustrated by a *New York Times* article claiming that the Democratic Party was "haunted by that tableau."[61] Yet what is haunting is not that the politicians were "hopelessly out of touch," as the article put it, but that they were enacting a charade (most of them were not actually against the camp), leaning into the political optics of a primary campaign rather than putting will behind those raised hands. When they (the Dems) caught the car and got into office, that commitment—both Biden and Harris had raised their hands—proved shallow. For our purposes here, the question is not how we return to that moment (we are at an even more urgent moment now) but how we get past that inflection point and regather lost momentum—not to trend another hashtag but to push to a place where nobody is locked up because of where they were born or where they move.

But closing camps, even closing all the camps, won't be enough. "What makes immigrants forever prisoners," writes historian Elliott Young in *Forever Prisoners*, "is not just the indeterminate time they spend locked up, but that they often remain vulnerable to detention and other forms of restrictions after release." Especially given the current globalized border regime, even after release, migrants "are never truly free."[62]

While communities can force the camps' closures, their specter may continue to haunt. We're seeing this now as the second Trump administration refurbishes recently shuttered or downsized camps such as Alabama's Etowah or Georgia's Irwin—both sites of exceptional cruelty. We've seen this before, with the repurposing of former Japanese internment camps to imprison migrants. The architecture of confinement, once built, exerts an inertial pull toward reactivation.

For the campaigners who understand their struggle in longer historical rhythms—from Reconstruction-era racial policing to the present convergence of immigration enforcement and mass incarceration—the lesson is unmistakable: To close a camp is not only to terminate a contract but to ensure the permanence of its obsolescence, whether through demolition, political covenant, or transformation into something wholly incapable of caging human beings. Or better: rebuilding a society that doesn't rely on camps. Only then can the dismantling of the carceral state become irreversible.

The camps' reopenings are a reminder that true abolition is based not in anti-politics or a carping opposition—one that rails facilely against the current administration—but in cultivating a positive vision of how we can do better. What can we build in place of the camp?

Translating a Movement

I spent almost a year in daily contact with Juan Castillo, a 41-year-old man from El Salvador, who was caged in ICE's Etowah camp in Alabama for five years. Juan would send me audio messages—via a contraband cell phone—describing his daily grind or imagining life for himself on the outside. The stories he and others shared, their resilience, their desire for freedom and dignity, are what fueled the campaign to shut down the camp. I reported his saga for *Latino USA*, and just weeks after we published, he was released.[63] Shortly afterward—the culmination of more than a decade of local organizing—ICE announced it would stop detaining migrants in Etowah.

The campaigns that have forced ICE out of jail wings and shuttered entire facilities offer a potential playbook for the first steps: document abuses closely with people inside; build durable relationships across bars and across faith and community groups; focus on contracts, licensing, and permitting vulnerabilities; and convert local moral outrage into national pressure. In Etowah County, organizers from Adelante and Detention Watch Network spent fourteen years recording medical neglect, prolonged solitary confinement, and pandemic-era mistreatment while maintaining steady lines of communication with those detained. That patient, yearslong relationship-driven organizing—regular visits, call-in campaigns, public vigils, and coordinated protests with national partners—helped make Etowah a liability for officials and ultimately led ICE, in 2022, to terminate its contract. The victory reduced the system's capacity and, crucially, was another example of how targeted local campaigns can win concrete closures.

The epilogue to Etowah's closure, however, is a story of backslide. In 2025, barely three years after the last detainees were transferred, local sheriffs and federal officials conspired to reopen the jail's cells to immigrant incarceration—a reminder that shutdown victories, absent structural guarantees or systemic change or repurposing, are fragile and reversible.[64]

I talked to Juan Castillo again shortly after the reopening of Etowah was announced. "Besides being heartbroken," he told me, "I started thinking about all those people who are going to go in there." Then he turned, as he often had when he was talking to me from the inside, to the food.

"The food," he said in what sounded like a mix between a sad cackle and a soulbroken sigh. "The food is just not edible. It's horrible. It shouldn't be fed to animals and they fed it to us, and they did it to punish us." I looked back at photos he had sent me from inside Etowah: a snapshot of dinner one night looked like a dog had vomited on the tray: protein meal and rice. I counted what looked like a couple grayish peas.

"It makes people desperate," Juan said. "It makes people with legitimate asylum cases say, 'You know what, I'd rather be facing danger than this place right here.' People I was in with signed their deportation papers and then we heard, a little while later, that they were dead."

Even while documenting the stomach-turning slop, the quotidian tortures and indignities, it's important not to overemphasize a distinction between the conditions and the camps themselves. Doing so suggests that reform can fix the camp. Michelle Castañeda, in her insightful study of immigrant detention and deportation, warns that succumbing to the logic of reform encourages observers "to be on the lookout for carceral atrocities while ignoring the atrocity of incarceration."[65] The problem, the crisis—the catastrophe at its core—is not what happens inside the camps. The catastrophe is the camp itself.

"The thing that resonates in the heart and mind," Juan told me of Etowah's reopening, "is heartbreak, loneliness, sadness."

■■■

The impacts of shutting down a camp reverberate beyond the physical structure. The yearslong effort to shutter the West County Detention Facility in California, for example, was successful, but the impact was mixed. While the camp itself was closed, people held in the facility were mostly transferred, not released. And yet, there were other effects, including a reduction in local immigration enforcement activity. A 2018 report, *Lessons from the ICE Detention Contract Termination in Contra Costa County, CA*, cites evidence "that fewer people from Northern California are now being detained. ICE itself has admitted as much, pointing to reductions in bed space as a 'challenge' to their operations." The finding "suggests closing detention facilities doesn't just redirect immigration detention; it actually bites away at it. Less bed space makes it harder to house, detain, and deport people."[66]

A separate study backs that claim: An immigrant is more than twice as likely to be arrested in a county with capacity to detain more than 50 people in ICE custody than in a county that has less or no camp capacity.[67] When a county has 850 or more detention beds, the likelihood of an immigrant being arrested is about six and a half times higher than if the county has none. Not only is the camp a danger to those inside of it; crucially, it is a constant threat to those outside of it as well.

If you don't want ICE prowling your neighborhood, it will help to close your neighborhood camp. If you don't want ICE prowling at all, close all the camps.

Showing Up

A CAMP IS A TRANS WOMAN FLEEING ABUSE AND LOCKED IN AN ALL-MALE PRISON WHERE SHE IS SEXUALLY ASSAULTED BY GUARDS, DENIED HORMONE MEDICATION, AND THROWN INTO SOLITARY CONFINEMENT WHEN SHE REPORTS HER ABUSE.[68]

A CAMP IS A MAN IN A WHEELCHAIR LOCKED IN A SHOWER AND LEFT UNDER RUNNING WATER AS PUNISHMENT.[69]

A CAMP IS A GUARD THREATENING TO USE AN ELECTRIFIED RIOT SHIELD TO SHOCK A WOMAN WHO IS NINE MONTHS PREGNANT.[70]

In the chapters that follow, I explain what a camp is, where camps came from, and why we need to shut them down, offering examples and lessons from campaigns to close them. I have learned much from the arguments and activism of people who have been in the camps, as well as those who have stood against or even stormed them—resisting, campaigning, blocking, monkey-wrenching, and refusing the camp, as well as imagining a world without them. I lean on the work of, among other groups, Detention Watch Network—an organization with a humble name, but which gives the verb *to watch* a potent political portent.

In the nearly two decades since the moral calamity of the border regime first snapped into focus for me, I have found what I believe is my most helpful role: as a reporter—recording abuses, holding the powerful to account, lifting up voices of those impacted, and helping to write, as they say, the first draft of history. But that designation, and this trade—journalism—even as it strives to disseminate information, push for accountability, and serves as a check on gross abuses of power, doesn't wholly fit. I think of myself first as a translator, my other vocation. I'm a translator who has borne witness to, and was briefly but proudly a part of, a movement that beautifully captures the power of human resilience and solidarity—the movement for migrant rights. That is the story I want to share, translating it from its innumerable particulars into something you can quickly read and act on in this time of escalating crisis. This book is the result of that act of translation.

My reporting and translating of the movement have made it clear to me that the opposite of a camp is community. The answer to how to close a camp is: You build community.

Or, as Juan put it to me, the way you close a camp is by "showing up."

PART I

WHAT THE CAMP BREAKS

1

"SAVAGE EXCLUSION"

THE HISTORY OF THE CAMP

The first camps were ships. Cramped, airless brigs creaking belowdecks as the tides and weather bobbed and yawed at their hulls. The food was meager and bad, sometimes turned. US government officials, bound or at least compelled by the Constitution, were responsible for protecting people within their jurisdiction—which meant that as soon as foreign passengers disembarked from a ship, they could avail themselves of the laws of the land. Yet if officials could keep those passengers off that land, so the logic went, they could avoid the lengthy or costly work of determining their immigration status.

And so, in the 1880s, US officials forced transoceanic ships to keep people on board—in those cramped and damp brigs—until they could be vetted. But that move was odious to the ships' captains, who could be forced to wait in the harbor for days or even weeks, feeding, maintaining, and dealing with the grief of their charges. It cut into company profits by delaying their next voyage. The passengers, unwanted from both sides, were crushed between the twin rocks of commerce and nationalism.

That tension, along with aggressive lobbying from shipping companies, pushed Congress to pass a law in 1891 defining a bizarre concept known as the "entry fiction," in which passengers could physically disembark from ships arriving to the United States but wouldn't be considered officially inside the country: Their entry, according to the state, was a fiction. They were on land but hadn't legally landed. Migrants consigned to this liminal space were held in buildings run by shipping companies, where the government could then process them and either let them in or try to send them back.

"A cheap, two-story wooden building, at the end of a wharf, built out over the water where the odors of sewage and bilge are most offensive": so describes one contemporary observer of a nineteenth-century dockside camp, quoted by scholar César Cuauhtémoc García Hernández in his book *Migrating to Prison: America's Obsession with Locking up Migrants*. "Unclean, at times overrun with vermin, and often inadequate to the numbers to be detained. The food provided was poor and the conditions even more unsanitary than the police cells of the city." An inspector called one such holding cell a "death trap."[1]

Thus was born an early iteration of the camp, what García Hernández calls "an in-between space in law . . . neither outside nor inside the United States."[2] The Kafkaesque duality still presides in the camps today: Immigration detention centers are not—by strict legal definition—punitive, and yet they are punishing. They are officially temporary but can be indefinite. They are administrative dungeons, exceptional and yet quotidian. The duality extends further still, to the two-faced nature of immigration politicking: Anti-immigrant factions (across the partisan divide) swear they don't want immigrants, or don't want too many immigrants, but our country depends on them to provide medical care, conduct scientific research, build homes, lay roads, open businesses, innovate, make art, and grow and cook food. Meanwhile, whole industries, namely the border and immigration enforcement industrial complexes, have developed because of them. Starker still is the paradox of politicians who vilify, scapegoat, cast all color of blame and hate on migrants and yet depend on them—at times for their very political raison d'être—for clickbait and campaign fodder. All of those contradictions, all those monstrosities, are embodied in the camp.

The bizarre buffer zone of the entry fiction lives on today in *zones d'attentes*, legal exception zones outside of strict territorial jurisdiction, such as those typically glass-walled passageways and waiting areas between international airport jetways and stale-air passport inspection halls.* The here-but-not-here reality inverts when nations render people stateless, pushing them off the edge of legal recognition and into an

* These zones are intentionally designed to dehumanize, to reduce people to biopolitical figures that can be assessed and screened. Architecture scholar Eyal Weizman details the border crossing turnstiles between the West Bank and Jerusalem: "People got stuck, parcels got crushed, dragged along and burst open on the ground. Heavier people got trapped in the narrow space, as were older women and mothers with small children." Eyal Weizman, *Hollow Land: Israel's Architecture of Occupation* (London: Verso, 2007).

omnipresent camp-like labyrinth of exclusion. Embodying such concocted logic are also nation-states—institutions that mark, define, exclude, and filter human beings—which are their own wide camps. The forms of the camp are many and often metastasize. None of them make sense, and yet they hurt and kill people. We could stop using them.

The Anti-Chinese Roots of the Modern Camp

The entry fiction solidified into US law a year before the 1892 passage of the Geary Act, which sparked a series of targeted crackdowns on Chinese Americans and created the first versions of what we often refer to today as "immigration detention centers." Written by Massachusetts Democrat Thomas Geary, the law required all Chinese people living in the United States to register with the federal government or be subject to arrest, up to one year imprisonment at hard labor, and then deportation.* As historian Kelly Lytle Hernández explains, "The act knotted immigration control to come and punishment in historically unprecedented and constitutionally questionable ways."[3] As we'll see, that knot has only been tightened over the subsequent 130 years.

---

* On his first day back in office, Trump signed an executive order establishing the Alien Registration Requirement for all migrants over the age of eighteen to keep evidence of registration "in their personal possession at all times." Immigration agents have already begun fining people, even legal permanent residents, for not keeping their papers on them at all times. Alexandra Markovich, "Border Patrol Now Targeting Legal Immigrants for 'Carry Your Papers' Law in Southern Arizona," Arizona Center for Investigative Reporting, March 4, 2026, https://azcir.org/news/2026/03/04/border-patrol-tickets-legal-immigrants-carry-your-papers/.

The fight over the Geary Act—and all the racism, jingoistic politicking, and treatment of foreigners as expendable labor that accompanied it—reached the Supreme Court twice, defining not only how, when, and under what authority immigrants could be deported, but how they could be caged in the process.

The Geary Act dovetailed neatly with the latest iteration of the Chinese Exclusion Act, passed the following day in May 1892, which prohibited all "Chinese laborers" from entering the US and reasserted that Chinese residents needed to have documents or they were subject to detention and deportation.[4]

The passage of both laws sparked swift resistance among Chinese Americans.* A group known as the Chinese Six Companies, a federation of organizations formerly advocating for the basic rights of Chinese in the United States, was perfectly primed to push back against the act—both in the courts and on the streets. A letter distributed by the Chinese Six urged all Chinese Americans to refuse to abide by the law, specifically in refusing to register or carry registration documents. The Chinese Six also asked every Chinese American in the country to contribute one dollar to its legal campaigns.

* Some lawmakers also objected: Representative Robert Hitt, a Republican from Illinois, fought hard against the act, proclaiming, "This savage exclusion and punishment of all strangers is a revival of the darkest features of the darkest ages in the history of man." Quoted in Alexander Jin, "'No Chinese Should Obey It': A Transpacific History of the Geary Act," *Pacific Historical Review* 94, no. 4 (2025): 374–408.

In an inspiring act of mass civil disobedience, hundreds of Chinese Americans willingly submitted to arrest with the strategic objective of overwhelming the courts. One official in San Francisco threatened not only to arrest any Chinese who protested but to detain them, developing the next facet of detention in the US—what would become known as "the Chinese Jail."

As immigration historian Brianna Nofil writes of the rise of such jails on the East Coast, "New York towns did not desire Chinese residents, but the Chinese prisoner filled a distinct social and economic role: his potential social threat had been neutralized by his lack of freedom, and his economic benefit outweighed his potential danger." Townspeople thought—as many still do today—they could make a buck by locking up immigrants. In New York State, marshals, sheriffs, attorneys, and others were getting paid—sometimes substantially—to hunt down, prosecute, and lock up Chinese migrants. Nofil notes that hundreds of people gathered outside some of these early camps, ogling and taking photos "in scenes reminiscent of spectators at a zoo."[5]

The Chinese Six's legal challenges led the Supreme Court to hold an emergency session in 1893 to hear the country's first-ever deportation case, *Fong Yue Ting v. United States*. With the decision, the court greenlit the Geary Act, also establishing that "deportation is not punishment for crime."[6] The ruling thus permitted federal deportation, defining forced removal as an administrative process. It also thrust deportation processes into that legally liminal space: If detention and deportation are civil matters and not considered punishment, then people subjected to them don't qualify for the same due process protections as those charged with criminal violations.

In another case with repercussions on detention, 1896's *Wong Wing v. United States*, the Supreme Court ruled that people ordered to be deported could not be summarily imprisoned or subjected to hard labor. The case also established that being in the country without documentation was not in itself a crime. That remains technically true today.*

The *Wong Wing* decision was issued on the same day as another infamous ruling, *Plessy v. Ferguson*, which gave legal imprimatur to white supremacy ("separate but equal accommodations for white and colored persons" under penalty of fines or imprisonment) and would remain a sanctioned legal practice for more than half a century. In *Plessy*'s lone dissent, Justice John Marshall Harlan argued against state-imposed racial divisions. "There is no caste here," he wrote of the United States. Yet, following anti-immigrant nativist logic, he still took a shot at the Chinese: "There is a race so different from our own that we do not permit those belonging to it to become citizens of the United States. Persons belonging to it are, with few exceptions, absolutely excluded from our country. I allude to the Chinese race."[7]

The blurred legal realm of the entry fiction and of "non-punitive" punishment—the tightrope the high court walked

---

* Not much remains known about Wong Wing himself, except that he crossed into the US from Canada, was poor, and was arrested—along with Lee Poy, Lee Yon Tong, and Chan Wan Dong—in Detroit on July 15, 1892, just two months after the passage of the Geary Act. A US commissioner sentenced them all to sixty days of hard labor followed by deportation to China. Within two weeks, a Detroit attorney, likely paid for by the Chinese Six, had already appealed to the Supreme Court, and shortly thereafter, Wong Wing was released on bail.

in *Wong Wing*—wedged open a legal space permitting immigration camps and erasing the legal boundaries between administrative detention and punishment. It created the immigration camp.

And that blurring implied—and still implies—minimal oversight and atrocious conditions. Compare the description from 130 years ago—the "death trap" conditions of the entry fiction camps "where the odors of sewage and bilge are most offensive"—to camp conditions today: "stagnant human waste has sat in sites across the facility and . . . people are resorting to desperate measures such as fasting in order to avoid defecating," according to one 2025 report from the Torrance County Detention Facility in New Mexico.[8] In 2023, the Innovation Law Lab published a report about Torrance, accompanied by a letter signed by 115 people detained in the camp calling for an investigation and its immediate closure.[9] The letter captured the same spirit of the Chinese Six's letter about the Geary Act 131 years earlier, which read: "No Chinese can read this law without a feeling of disgust."

In a case of such disgust from Florida, also from 2025, guards made hungry men eat with their hands shackled behind their backs. One man said: "We had to bend over and eat off the chairs with our mouths, like dogs."[10]

These are the dungeon conditions permitted by legal fudging, by justices, lawmakers, presidents, and the public permitting the camp to exist. And while the prison ships and the Geary Act were the beginning, there were other critical maneuverings that built up, solidified, and weaponized camp architecture—an architecture that can't be disassembled without understanding its archetypal blueprints.

As abolitionist thinker and polestar Ruth Wilson Gilmore wrote of the rapid rise of the prison industrial complex in California, we must consider "the dynamics of the social and spatial interactions where [prison] expansion emerged."[11]

"Loneliness in the Wooden Building"

While official history mainly remembers the storied Ellis Island Immigration Station as a site of welcome, it also served as an immigrant detention camp. Opened in 1892, it became the central immigration entry point for migrants on the East Coast. Yet over the decades it was in operation, its role shifted from one of processing entries to one of facilitating exclusion. In 1907, the busiest year in the island's history—with over one million people passing through the island that year—10 percent of all arriving migrants were held in detention. That's more than one hundred thousand people locked up over the course of a single year. Ten years later, in 1917, Ellis Island could accommodate up to two thousand detainees at any one time.

One woman, Ellen Knauff, writing in 1948, described her first view of the station: "I could see that parts of it were enclosed by double wire fences topped by barbed wire and marked by what appeared to be watchtowers. These fenced-off areas were subdivided by more fences which gave the whole place the look of a group of kennels." Knauff, who would have known about the possibility of being kept in one of the kennels, might have been worried that she would be detained like the Japanese, Germans, and Italians before her. Referencing a *New York Times* article from two years earlier, she called Ellis Island "a concentration camp with steam heat and running water."[12]

Meanwhile, on the West Coast, Angel Island Immigration Station in San Francisco Bay and McNeil Island in Washington State offered a similar unwelcome to immigrants arriving from Asia. Opened as a quarantine station in the late nineteenth century, Angel Island was the site where new arrivals, mostly Chinese, were subjected to medical examinations, inspection of legal documentation, and extensive interrogations before they were allowed (or denied) entry into the US. Many were detained for months while they awaited a hearing; if they were denied entry, they could appeal before they were deported, but that could mean spending up to two years locked up. Between 1910 and 1940, the government held around three hundred thousand migrants on the island.[13]

Chinese immigrants detained on Angel Island formed mutual aid associations to support each other. They also recorded their experiences of detention by writing or carving hundreds of poems on the walls of the barracks during the three decades the island operated as a detention camp. "Instead of remaining a citizen of China, I willingly became an ox," one poem begins. Another migrant, calling the center a prison, writes: "One cannot bear to ask about the loneliness in the wooden building."[14]

The poems from Angel Island aren't the only literary lights produced in the early camps. C. L. R. James, Trinidadian revolutionary thinker and author of *The Black Jacobins*, was detained for four months on Ellis Island in 1952. There he wrote a brilliant exegesis of Herman Melville's *Moby Dick*, in which he captured what he saw as the spirit of America. In *Mariners, Renegades and Castaways*, James argued the United States, while claiming to be a bastion of liberty and democracy, enforces conformity and class hierarchy, all while crushing dissent through bureaucratic machinery. James saw *Moby Dick* as a parable of an authoritarian order disguised as a collective enterprise, much like the US immigration system hidden within the melting-pot mythos. "Overweening national arrogance sweeping over the world like some pestilence," James observed of the country. "I was an alien. I had no human rights."[15]

James's confinement was not an isolated case but part of a pattern of racist and ideological targeting established decades earlier. The US was ostensibly responding to a "crisis" of domestic communist threats, but in reality the crisis served as both excuse and opportunity. It was a "pretextual moment," to invoke political scientist Corey Robin's term for such moments of crackdowns.[16] The weapon was ready and loaded—the state was just awaiting an excuse to fire. The camp system thus served as an ideological and racial filter—as experienced by James, Knauff, and the Chinese—and a means of increasing the costs (not only financial but physical and emotional) of migration: a tool of controlling labor, as would become a central function of the camp, especially in the targeting of Mexicans in the second half of the twentieth century.

The "Internment" of Enemies and Subversives

Two months after Japan attacked the US naval base at Pearl Harbor on December 7, 1941, President Roosevelt signed Executive Order 9066, enabling the War Department to forcibly remove and detain close to 120,000 Japanese citizens and residents of Japanese descent living in the western United States. Initially, they were taken to temporary "assembly centers"—fairgrounds, horse racetracks, stockyards, and other spaces hastily converted to detention camps while the War Relocation Authority built facilities, officially called "relocation centers," for long-term detention. The camps were located in less populated areas throughout the West and Southeast. Their barracks-style housing was surrounded by barbed wire fences, with armed guards surveilling the camps from watchtowers.*

By the mid-1940s the Immigration and Naturalization Service (INS) was running at least sixty-five different internment camps. And while many think it was merely a reaction to the deadly attack on Pearl Harbor, it had in fact been years earlier that Roosevelt first raised the possibility of building concentration camps to detain Japanese immigrants and Japanese Americans. Tens of thousands of Japanese had migrated to Hawaii by the early twentieth century, many recruited to work on the islands' sugar plantations. Protests and strikes organized by Japanese, Filipino, and Puerto Rican laborers at the time led to increased government surveillance and plans to discipline these immigrant communities—and a key tool

---

* In addition to the relocation camps run by the War Relocation Authority, during World War II the Department of Justice established INS-administered camps to detain Japanese, German, and Italian nationals; Japanese and German POWs; as well as Germans, Italians, and Japanese living in Latin America. Begun in Panama because of ostensible security concerns around the Panama Canal, the Latin America deportation program saw Japanese residents there and in other countries arrested and turned over to US authorities. They were then sent to detention camps in the US. The camps run by the Justice Department detained over 2,200 people of Japanese ancestry from twelve Latin American countries.

for such discipline was the camp. Suspicious in particular of Japanese residents communicating with Japanese ships in Hawaiian ports, as noted by Gary Okihiro in *Encyclopedia of Japanese Internment*, Roosevelt suggested the military create "a special list of those who would be the first to be placed in a concentration camp in the event of trouble."[17]

In 1936—still years before World War II began—Roosevelt inquired: "What arrangements and plans have been made relative to concentration camps in the Hawaiian Islands for dangerous or undesirable aliens or citizens in the event of national emergency?"[18]

It's important to emphasize there was no grounds for detention—no evidence they posed a threat—other than racism. Regardless of citizenship, Japanese people in the US were labeled en masse as "enemy aliens"—identifying them as a population subject to detention under the guise of military necessity. A grandson of one of the detained, contemporary poet Brandon Shimoda, writes, "Japanese immigrants and Japanese Americans were forced from their homes and incarcerated in concentration camps during World War II *for nothing*. The dispossession and dehumanization of an entire population—approximately 125,284 Japanese and Okinawan immigrants and American citizens; the violence and pain, suffering and loss; the innumerable lifetimes of hauntedness: *nothing*."[19] Still: wholesale roundup of families, including children and the elderly. They were forced to sell homes, cars, and property as they were evacuated into camps. Frank Sumida, the son of one man who was dispossessed of his San Francisco restaurant, recalled that they were "never compensated. Not a penny." He said restaurant wholesalers were waiting outside the door for the family to be shipped off to the camp, which is when "they just go right in there [the restaurant] and steal everything. They won't buy it. They knew we were going into camp, so why buy it when you could get it free? And that's what they did."*[20]

■■■

The end of World War II marked a rhetorical shift in federal immigration policy, in part to differentiate detention practices in the US from the concentration camps of the defeated Nazis. It was also part of a geopolitical strategy in the emergent Cold War with the Soviet Union, as American legal theorist Mary Dudziak has shown, in which the US wanted to portray a more inclusive approach by ending outright exclusion of Asian immigrants.[21] At the same time, however, it targeted and increased screenings and surveillance of potential Communists or anyone advocating "world communism." At a naturalization ceremony in November 1954, for example, US Attorney General Herbert Brownell Jr. announced, "In all but a few cases, those aliens whose admissibility or deportation is under study will no longer be detained. All others will be released on conditional parole or bond or supervision."[22]

And yet, despite the public posturing of a more liberal immigration policy and the closing of some detention centers, the detention and deportation infrastructure did not shrink during the era; rather, the sites of concentration and the communities that were targeted shifted. In 1952, Congress passed the Immigration and Nationality Act

* In 1988, the Civil Liberties Act granted surviving Japanese Americans who were interned in the camp $20,000 and an apology.

(the McCarran-Walter Act), which targeted immigrants suspected of subversive political activity and drug use and authorized the INS to deport anarchists, Communists, and members of other subversive organizations, along with "narcotic drug addicts." Amid the growing anti-Communist paranoia fueling political rhetoric of the time, journalists and politicians claimed that Communists were entering the country disguised as farmworkers.* Six months before his claim, in 1954, that the US would curtail the detention of immigrants, Brownell—in response to rising nativism and largely misdirected economic anxiety—announced "Operation Wetback," a campaign to round up, detain, and deport Mexican immigrants. Operation Wetback intensified both the racialization and criminalization of migrants, effectively marking all Mexicans as drug addicts, political subversives, or somehow dangerous.

Overall, in 1954, the INS detained 508,566 people in detention camps throughout the country, the highest number of immigrant prisoners at that point. According to Jessica Ordaz's study *The Shadow of El Centro: A History of Migrant Incarceration and Solidarity*, in just the last six months of 1954, the INS detained 52,855 migrants at McAllen detention camp, some for a few hours and others for several months, before they were deported.[23] Overcrowding and abuse were nearly constant, as noted by federal inspectors, journalists, and others visiting these camps. According to the INS, some 1.3 million Mexicans were apprehended and deported as a result of the Operation Wetback campaign.

---

* C. L. R. James said the McCarran bill was "permeated with the doctrine of racial superiority."

In this same period, Nofil writes, "the United States took the technology and spaces developed in wartime—the internment camps and jails—and turned them toward policing Mexican migrants: men, women and children whom the United States deemed surplus labor."[24] The war came home: The same planes paratroopers jumped from during the war began airlifting deportees, and factories that had churned out Jeeps and tanks were converted to detention camps. The use of immigration laws, as historian Mae Ngai writes in *Impossible Subjects*, also reaffirmed the racialized focus of enforcement: naturalizing the concept of "illegal migrant" and pinning it to Mexicans.[25] Despite the softer rhetoric, the camp was still being used as a selective tool of human sorting—much like the border—for population control.

The Prison Boom

Immigration detention as we know it in the 2020s was constructed atop the scaffolding of the late twentieth century's embrace of mass incarceration—the primary response to what politicians, policymakers, and prison companies alike called the "wars" on crime and drugs. In the 1980s, the Reagan administration launched both rhetorical and legislative campaigns that fused criminal justice with immigration enforcement, entangling immigrants in a rapidly pullulating carceral system.

And while the 1980s and '90s are rightly remembered as the lit fuse of mass incarceration, the militarization of local law enforcement had begun a decade earlier as a fear response to the civil rights uprisings, with migrants always sharing the crosshairs. The Safe Streets Act of 1968, along with the increased use of immigration "detainers," locked up more migrants in local jails, where they were held for increasingly lengthy periods and then turned over to INS. The 1960s and '70s, not coincidentally, witnessed the increased arrival of darker-skinned migrants from Haiti and Cuba, as well as the rise of permanent migration from Mexico.

In 1977, Leonel Castillo, the first Latino INS commissioner, changed the term "alien detention centers" to "service processing centers." The softened language didn't close the camps but, rather, whitewashed their purpose. What had been beta tested in the 1950s and '60s against Mexicans in the Southwest, mostly for short-term periods, metastasized into a sprawling infrastructure of extended and brutal confinement.

The convergence of racist, punitive practices of "criminal justice" and anti-immigration restrictions intensified in the spring of 1980. In March, as an increasing number of Haitians began making their way to Florida to seek asylum, the INS leased a facility in Miami, the Federal Correction Institution, from the Bureau of Prisons. That took place the same month that the Refugee Act was signed into law, establishing the modern era of asylum processing, which, on the books, functions as a means of uniformly vetting asylum claims but has long been used as a legal shield for the selective denial of asylum claims.

Then, beginning in April, more than 125,000 Cubans migrated across the Florida Strait in a matter of months in what became known as the Mariel boatlift.*

---

* A historical moment I address at length in my previous book, *The Case for Open Borders* (Haymarket Books, 2024).

The carceral response to these so-called Marielitos that followed, as well as to the arrival of Cubans in search of asylum in subsequent years, would help cement a pattern of US officials blaming migrants for the misery the US was inflicting. To house the targets of its newest nativist campaign, the INS opened detention camps in Florida, Arkansas, and Pennsylvania and repurposed facilities in Arizona and Georgia, in a move that was less a response to criminality than a creation of the *perception of crime*. Officials launched a punitive immigration crackdown, then, when migrants and advocates called out their abuses—and sometimes revolted—they relied on yet further criminal enforcement. Initially, the Cubans were going to be held in camps for days or weeks, but those weeks stretched into months. By the summer of 1980, nearly half of the Marielitos were held on military bases.

As the Cuban refugees were dispersed throughout various states, local residents, including members of the Ku Klux Klan, protested. In May 1980, the Air Force fire hosed Cubans protesting their confinement at Florida's Fort Eglin. The next month, at Arkansas's Fort Chaffee, federal police fired live rounds at refugees protesting their detention. A new category of migrant was thus established during the period: the so-called hardcore refugee.*

Florida's response pushed many of the newly arrived Cubans into precarity and prison, where officials separated families, held women and young children in extended and abusive conditions, and otherwise made it hard at every turn for refugees to find their footing. Municipalities passed

* The term would echo in the next decade with the concept of the "superpredator."

emergency laws that criminalized homelessness, establishing a revolving door between local jails and Dade County streets. Meanwhile, from 1980 to 1985, the Miami Police Department nearly doubled in size.

As refugees became a national political flash point, a 1981 memo from Reagan's attorney general, prepared for his "Task Force on Immigration and Refugee Policy," weighed the pros and cons of reliance on the camp as means of deterrence.* The memo noted that a policy of detention would be favorably viewed by those in favor of strict enforcement. "The location of large detention facilities, however, would be politically sensitive. Liberals, minorities, and church groups would oppose these measures as draconian and, they may say, racist." Another con was that the "policy of detention presents risk that camps would overflow because of procedural delays in exclusion hearings."[26] The concern was prescient; today the number of backlogged immigration cases approaches four million.

Most disturbingly, another listed con was that "the appearance of 'concentration camps' which, at the present time, would be filled largely by blacks, may be publicly unacceptable." After the deliberation, Reagan issued an order to interdict all unauthorized migrants coming by sea.

Even while the Reagan administration was increasingly targeting migrants, the approach to immigration was still not exclusively exclusionary. The 1986 Immigration Reform and Control Act, often remembered as the "amnesty bill," "legalized" around three million immigrants living in the

---

* The task force was chaired by the attorney general and his deputy, Rudolph W. Giuliani.

United States, including some of my family members. But the bill contained some poison pills, including criminalizing the hiring of undocumented workers, which effectively deputized employers to police job candidates. Also in that bill was a provision that authorized the use of immigration "detainers," which allowed INS to request that local law enforcement hold immigrants accused of certain crimes until they could be transferred to INS custody. In other words, at the same time they granted pathways to citizenship to millions, they set others on the path to dedocumentation and deportation.

The so-called wars on drugs and crime tended to include laws that specifically targeted migrants. The Anti–Drug Abuse Act of 1986, for instance, concocted the concept of "aggravated felony," a type of crime that, when committed by a noncitizen, typically leads to mandatory detention. It also allowed for the exclusion or deportation of any migrant who violated *any* drug law.

Another key moment of camp expansion came when the Reagan administration launched the Cooperative Agreement Program, which paid local governments to build jails in exchange for guarantees the feds could use the jail space. Over twenty years of the program, the federal government doled out over a quarter billion dollars for communities to increase jail capacity. By the end of the 1980s, policymakers had reframed the camp not as an extraordinary measure but as a routine fact of immigration processing.

The Prison-Immigration Knot

By the late 1980s, thanks to over a decade of laws criminalizing immigrants and expanding the camp system, prison and immigration detention industries were operating by their own economic logics. Even in the face of recessions, the prison industry kept growing. Immigration detention was seen by the Reagan administration as "recession-proof."[27] For private corporations like CoreCivic (formerly Corrections Corporation of America), founded in 1983, immigration detention was a financial lifeline. Federal contracts insulated companies from state budget crises and guaranteed steady revenue streams.

Detention was sold as both a law-and-order necessity and an economic opportunity, welding together the racist politics of the drug war with the rise of private prisons. Communities hollowed out by deindustrialization welcomed detention centers as employers of last resort. Local politicians who couldn't secure new factories or union jobs instead competed for prisons and INS contracts. Officials in Port Isabel, Texas, for instance, saw the expansion of what was known as El Corralón, or "the big corral," as a way to cash in on Reagan's willingness to lock up asylum seekers.

But if Reagan set the foundation, the Clinton administration built the superstructure. Clinton rode into office pledging to be tough not only on crime but also on immigrants. Governor of Arkansas at the time of the Mariel boatlift, he was furious at the Jimmy Carter administration for detaining migrants at an Arkansas camp. The political backlash had been costly for him, and his resentment carried into his presidency. Clinton's 1994 crime bill funneled billions into prison construction and policing, while his 1996 immigration laws fundamentally reshaped the landscape of enforcement. The Antiterrorism and Effective Death Penalty Act and the Illegal Immigration Reform and Immigrant

Responsibility Act expanded the categories of deportable offenses, introduced mandatory detention for a wide range of crimes (including minor and decades-old convictions), and sharply curtailed judicial discretion. The antiterrorism law, ostensibly in response to the most homegrown of terror acts (especially the 1995 Oklahoma City bombing by white nationalist Timothy McVeigh), in fact focused on purported threats coming from abroad. The law changed the detention of many migrants from discretionary to mandatory, allowing migrants to be detained for up to two years before seeing an immigration judge.

The 1996 laws, the "aggravated felony" category introduced in 1988, and the expansion of INS camps like Krome in Miami and Port Isabel in Texas marked the complete insertion of immigration detention into the American carceral state. Now, the same logic that incarcerated millions of Black Americans under mandatory minimums and three-strikes laws also ensnared migrants—justified by the same political rhetoric of danger, disorder, and deterrence. Both carceral outgrowths served the same economic interests of private prison companies and, purportedly, struggling rural economies. And both entrenched a culture of disposability, where human beings were warehoused in the name of public safety.

The expansion of the immigration camp system was rapid and dramatic. In 1994, there were fewer than 7,000 immigrants in detention on any given day. By 2001, the INS was detaining an average of 19,500 noncitizens daily, with nearly 190,000 detained over the course of that fiscal year. And while the expansion was sold to localities as an economic windfall, the promise was empty. Researchers Amy Glasmeier and Tracey Farrigan compared fifty-five rural counties with prisons constructed between 1985 and 1995 to similar counties without prisons. They found "little evidence of prisons fostering economic growth especially in persistently poor communities."[28] As the "century of the camp" began to sunset, the prison industrial complex, reverting to the same dehumanizing divisiveness, had become a catchall political solution.

■■■

The course was set in the 1990s, but, as they did for so much else, the September 11, 2001 terrorist attacks marked another key inflection point for immigration camps. In one of the first immigration enforcement moves after the towers fell, INS Acting Deputy Commissioner Peter Michael Becraft implemented a new parole policy targeting Haitian asylum seekers: No Haitian could be paroled out of detention without direct approval from INS headquarters in Washington, even if they had proven their eligibility for asylum. As migrant justice organizer Silky Shah tells me, "Anti-Black racism is the underlying component of the rise of these anti-immigrant systems." 9/11 also prompted the creation of the Department of Homeland Security and its subagency ICE.

Many such senseless, vindictive, and downright racist policies would follow, such as the PATRIOT Act, allowing for indefinite detention, or the 2004 Intelligence Reform and Terrorism Prevention Act, which mandated ICE increase detention capacity by eight thousand per year from 2006 to 2010.

From the inception of his administration in 2000, George W. Bush oversaw a massive expansion of border militarization, including hundreds of miles of border barriers and doubling the number of Border Patrol agents. The vilification, scapegoating, surveillance, and arrests of Muslims, in particular, presaged the open revilement cast on Haitians and other darker-skinned migrants during the Trump administration. At the same time, looking at either the Clinton presidency before Bush or Obama's presidency after highlights the bipartisan reliance on the camp. In 2009, Democratic Senator Robert Byrd from West Virginia introduced a clause in the DHS Appropriations Bill that the department "shall maintain a level of not less than 33,400 detention beds."[29] In 2012, that "bed quota," as it became known, was raised to 34,000. The federal government pays out contracts for those beds—via the so-called "guaranteed minimum" clauses—whether they're filled or not.

On the state level, Arizona, followed by both Georgia and Alabama, led the way in 2010 by trying to make unauthorized migration not only a federal crime but also a state violation. The hypocrisy of crackdown culture continued: All three states passed harsh anti-immigrant laws at the same time they courted ICE contracts to open new detention centers, meaning local jurisdictions increasingly depended on detaining the very people they wanted out.[30]

The experience of detention in Georgia's Irwin County highlights the local effects of that dependency. What had been a US Marshals facility in the rural county in the early 1990s had shut down. In 2004, a private company reopened the facility to serve as an overflow lockup, detaining people from other counties. With the economy in Irwin struggling—a drought and a lack of migrant agricultural workers were making things worse—in 2007, the county passed a

$55 million bond package to expand the prison. They were hoping to attract federal agencies in the detention business and turn the prison into the county's lifeline. It didn't quite work. There simply wasn't enough revenue, and by 2011, after another change in ownership, the facility was nearly a million dollars behind on its taxes. As reported in *The Nation*, Hazel McCranie, president of the Ocilla-Irwin Chamber of Commerce, told local officials: "You've got to go out and get a contract with ICE. That's your salvation."[31]

To entice ICE, the joint owners of the prison, with the support of members of Congress and former Senator Johnny Isakson, offered a deal: Instead of spending the typical $60, $90, or sometimes over $160 per day to lock a person up, ICE could cage someone in the Irwin camp for only forty-five dollars a day. ICE soon began transferring people from Alabama's Etowah jail (where, as we saw in the introduction, Juan was locked up for almost five years) to Irwin.

In January 2011, four people locked inside the Irwin camp went on hunger strike and were sent to solitary confinement as punishment. One detained person held in the Irwin camp, Florent Firmin Kalonji Kalala, told reporters, "We're fed like dogs." He added: "I just feel humiliated—that's the feeling I have every day."[32]

Years later, the county's moral and financial compromise deepened. In 2020, reporter José Olivares and I broke a story about Irwin that made international headlines: Besides dangerously lax protocols amid the COVID-19 pandemic, an ICE-contracted doctor who treated patients at Irwin was multiply accused of performing invasive, nonconsensual, and unnecessary gynecological surgeries. We spoke with one woman, Yuridia, who was held in the camp and went to see the doctor after suffering lower abdominal cramps.[33] Without proper explanation, she was soon on the operating table. It wasn't until she was deported to Mexico that, still suffering the after-effects of the surgery, she learned she had had her uterus removed.

Once exposed, the conditions prompted international outcry, lawsuits, and a Senate investigation, while giving more fuel to people inside and out fighting to shut down the camp. In 2021, ICE announced it was closing the Irwin camp. Then, just as we've seen time and again with other camps that aren't demolished or turned into something new, in 2025 the Trump administration announced its reopening. Steady source of tax revenue, reliable employer, wholesome community partner the camp is not.

Much of the camp infrastructure we see today was established in the Obama years. In 2014, as more families, mostly from Central America, fled violence and poverty and headed toward the United States, the Obama administration—following the encrusted playbook first written in the nineteenth century to try to dispel the Chinese—reverted to using detention as an attempted means of deterrence. First they reoutfitted a law enforcement training site in Artesia, New Mexico; then, they opened the 2,400-bed South Texas Family Residential Center in Dilley, Texas, to lock up mothers and their children. In 2015 I spent a week in and out of the camp in Dilley—then one of the largest detention camps in the country—frequently referred to as a "baby jail."*

* To underscore the shady and sometimes diabolically twisted nature of the procurement process: ICE contracted the Dilley family camp not directly through CoreCivic, or the town of Dilley, or

Though school-age kids attended classes inside Dilley and had ready access to milk and apples—adding a thin veneer of humanism to the camp—the atmosphere was starkly punitive. Many of the children I met had colds or coughs. Medical attention was slow and, according to women I interviewed, sick kids were regularly told by medical staff simply to drink water. This was the same tap water that a cook at a local drive-thru taco shop told me not to drink "cuz of the oil"—a reference to the fact that residents in and around Dilley were concerned about fracking wastewater contaminating their groundwater. Many of the kids had trouble sleeping, and women I spoke with reported that their children were depressed and not eating. One told me that her 11-year-old boy had lost more than ten pounds since coming to Dilley. "We are creating a mental health crisis," one attorney representing the moms and kids, and working to shut the place down, said. "These kids are going to have PTSD and need serious therapy."

The same year, in 2014, the Obama administration also opened an ICE staging facility in Alexandria, Louisiana: a camp with an airport, allowing for more efficient deportations. As Nora Ahmed, the director of ACLU Louisiana,

---

Frio County in Texas, but the small town of Eloy, Arizona, which was nine hundred miles away and had been contracting with ICE for a separate camp since 2006. The Arizona town took in nearly half a million dollars a year acting as ICE's middleman. US Department of Homeland Security, Office of Inspector General, *Immigration and Customs Enforcement Did Not Follow Federal Procurement Guidelines When Contracting for Detention Services*, OIG-18-53, February 21, 2018, https://www.oig.dhs.gov/sites/default/files/assets/2018-02/OIG-18-53-Feb18.pdf.

explained to me, the facility was "really what allowed Obama to become the deporter-in-chief." (In the Trump era, the cruel efficiency of the Obama administration's camp-airport infrastructure has proven incredibly useful.)

Protests, hunger strikes, shutdown campaigns—all of it pushed the Obama administration to issue cosmetic changes and scale back some of the most dehumanizing excesses of the camp system. While Dilley was finally shuttered in 2024, the following year the Trump administration announced it was reopening it.[34] A few months later, a legal complaint detailed how young children held in the Dilley family camp, sometimes for months, did not have reliable access to clean drinking water, soap, or shampoo. The echoes of 2015—nearly identical human rights complaints coming out of the same camp—were clamorous. Parents and their young children reported sleep deprivation due to lights being on 24/7 and a lack of emergency medical attention for kids in acute medical distress. One 11-year-old girl wrote to her attorneys, "Sometimes I see kids who are sad. Most of the kids don't play because they are afraid."[35] One nine-year-old boy regressed so severely he could no longer control his bowel movements and had to start using diapers.

Kids who don't play, diapers on nine-year-olds—this is Clinton, Obama, and Biden's immigration policy legacy: building out the camp infrastructure to humiliate, starve, abuse, and lay the groundwork for their virulently anti-immigrant successors.

And yet there are ways—long established and newly dusted off, storied and hardly recognized—to push back. It can start with simply questioning the legitimacy of the camps.

A fascinating 1993 Department of Justice report, *Resolution of Prison Riots*, mentioned Cuban migrants protesting their detention and included a section called "Breakdown of Legitimacy of Imprisoning Criteria," which notes:

> We observe that most inmates most of the time accept as legitimate the imprisonment of their fellow inmates. They may protest their own conviction or sentence but, at the same time, believe that the other inmates are guilty of crimes, deserve prison sentences, and ought not to be discharged en masse. In uncommon periods in history, however, these beliefs may be challenged. Once it is held that the criteria for imprisonment are arbitrary, it is a short step to the belief that rebellion is justified.[36]

In other words, if we recognize the arbitrariness of imprisoning people because of where they are from or where they have moved, we begin to see through the illusion of the camp. We are in such an "uncommon" period now. We can see through the illusion, and we can take that short step toward rebellion against the camp.

1941 to 2026

Eighty years ago, the military base Fort Bliss, outside of El Paso, held Japanese immigrants and Japanese Americans under the 1798 Alien Enemies Act. Families were uprooted, branded "enemy aliens," and herded into compounds ringed by barbed wire despite, as one researcher put it, "no accounts of wrongdoing" except their ancestry.[37] That history echoes in today's sprawling white-tent detention camp—capacity five thousand—reopened in 2025 on the same ground in Fort Bliss, this time under the banner of MAGA-style immigration enforcement.*

What is happening in the 2020s is not metaphorical repetition of the 1940s but structural continuity: Mass arrests, indefinite confinement, and the deployment of military infrastructure to suppress "undesirable" populations. Mike Ishii, whose family endured the Minidoka concentration camp in Idaho during the Japanese internment era, sees the same frightening pattern from eighty years ago—immigration raids ripping people from homes, workplaces, hospitals, and schools. Ishii, who is also the executive director and cofounder of Tsuru for Solidarity, an immigrant rights advocacy group, told reporters, "Right now, it's very frightening for people. In 1941, it was also frightening."[38]

DHS has insisted any such comparison is "deranged and lazy," at the same time they vilify people they round up, going so far as establishing an official government website to name

---

* In less than two months in the hastily (re)erected camp on Fort Bliss, three migrants died, one of them allegedly choked to death by guards. An inspection found the camp was violating at least sixty federal standards for immigrant detention. Douglas MacMillan, "DHS Seeking to Deport Two Men Who Said Fellow ICE Detainee Was Killed," *Washington Post*, January 17, 2026, https://www.washingtonpost.com/immigration/2026/01/17/detainee-death-witnesses-deported-dhsa/; Douglas MacMillan et al., "60 Violations in 50 Days: Inside ICE's Giant Tent Facility at Ft. Bliss," *Washington Post*, September 16, 2025, https://www.washingtonpost.com/business/2025/09/16/ice-detention-center-immigration-violations/.

and shame people they call "the worst of the worst." The euphemisms shift—"enemy alien" in 1941, "illegal alien" in 2025—but the machinery is familiar: anti-"foreigner" ideology instilled, camps quickly erected, due process suspended, and racialized bodies warehoused out of public sight.

2

THE TOLL OF THE CAMP

A CAMP IS A PREGNANT WOMAN IN ACTIVE LABOR AND DELIRIOUS WITH PAIN WHO BORDER PATROL AGENTS TELL TO SIT DOWN AND "WAIT TO BE PROCESSED." HER DAUGHTERS AND TWENTY STRANGERS, ALL LOCKED INTO THE SAME HOLDING CELL, LOOK ON.[1]

A CAMP IS A MAN SARDINED INTO AN "ICEBOX"—THE FREEZING, BEDLESS, LIGHTS-ON-24/7 BORDER PATROL HOLDING FACILITIES—STARVING AND SWARMED BY FLEAS. TAUNTING GUARDS TELL HIM THE BUGS LIKE HIS FILTH, THAT HE'S BETTER OFF THAN HE WOULD BE AT HOME.[2]

A CAMP IS A MAN WITH A MENTAL DISABILITY WHO IS TOLD TO SIGN A FORM IF HE WANTS TO RECEIVE A BLANKET AND THEN IS DEPORTED AFTER "CONSENTING TO VOLUNTARY DEPARTURE."[3]

A CAMP IS A WOMAN WHO SLIPS A NOTE TO A FELLOW DETAINEE, INVITING HIM TO JOIN A HUNGER STRIKE.[4]

One day in May 2019, after spending two months in an immigration camp in Eloy, Arizona, guards found Beto in the yard in the fetal position, "shaking, tearful, paranoid." Beto (a pseudonym) later reported to a social worker that he was "hearing a lot of voices yelling at him to throw himself off the second tier of the ward where he was detained," according to an official complaint filed by his attorneys.

A psychiatrist working for CoreCivic prescribed Beto risperidone, a medicine used to treat schizophrenia and bipolar disorder. The doctor ordered him to be placed on suicide watch in a segregation unit, meaning he would be almost entirely isolated—his only interaction with others the occasional welfare check or food delivery from the guards.

With mere minutes of human contact each day, Beto's condition quickly deteriorated. Medical records cited in the complaint say that he began laughing and smiling "inappropriately," that he had a "wide and blank stare," that he would rub his body against the wall. He heard voices saying they were going to kill him. He dealt with hallucinations "constantly," often seeing a color-changing bird flitting around his cell or tending to an imaginary cricket in his sink. On June 18, Beto tried to kill himself.

Medical records note that there were marks on Beto's neck from where he had tried to hang himself, but he had not been taken to the hospital. He told medical staff that "he felt like he was in a dream and not reality." By that point, he was spending most of his time completely naked.

On July 4, a psychiatrist noted that the use of constant isolation "could potentially worsen his mental state and even contribute to his non-improvement." And yet staff again placed Beto on suicide watch, warehousing him completely alone.

At the end of July, Beto again attempted to kill himself, tying one end of a sheet around his neck and the other end around the top of a bunk bed. According to the complaint, the guard who first saw him responded by pepper-spraying him in the face. Staff then transported him to the hospital.

Finally, on August 2, after three months in solitary, Beto was taken to Cornerstone, a specialty hospital in Tucson about an hour away, where he stayed until August 21. Doctors at the hospital diagnosed him with schizophrenia and transported him back to the detention center. Again guards in the facility placed him, alone, on suicide watch.

None of these suicide attempts were counted in the 2019 annual inspection review conducted by a third-party, nongovernmental inspector, the Nakamoto Group. Nakamoto's inspection of Eloy Detention Center found that in 2019, there were "no serious suicide attempts during the inspection period."[5] And yet ICE's own incident reports, obtained by attorney Andrew Free, recorded eleven suicide attempts in the same camp in 2019. The ineffectiveness of ICE's inspections of their own facilities, or the inspections they contract out to third parties, has long been a point of contention and consternation among immigration activists, as well as another factor deepening the suffering of those inside.

That glaring discrepancy was indicative of a broader and deadly problem. Attorneys and immigration advocates say that the lack of proper monitoring has led conditions in ICE facilities to spiral into a situation where people detained are denied even basic medical and mental health care, left to languish in squalid and sometimes deadly conditions. By 2025, concerns about pro forma, often-futile inspections were temporarily rendered moot when the two subagencies charged with such oversight—the Office for Civil Rights and Civil Liberties and the Office of the Immigration Detention Ombudsman—were abolished by the Trump administration: The illusion of oversight was over. A lawsuit reestablished them later in the year, but inspections and oversight reports became a rarity. Camps started to refuse access to elected officials, even concerned members of Congress. In July 2025, Yassamin Ansari, a freshman congressional representative from Phoenix, tried to access the Eloy camp and was turned away.[6] Ansari had gone to Eloy because one of her constituents, Arbella "Yari" Rodríguez Márquez, was locked inside and denied proper treatment for leukemia.

Yari, who had lived in Phoenix for twenty-five years, was arrested by ICE in February 2025. A year later, she had lost over seventy pounds and had begun to vomit blood every day. Ansari made it into the camp twice but was also once denied access and, despite advocating for Yari, saw no improvement in her care. "The medical care she has received—sporadic vitamins, Tylenol, and ulcer medication—does not begin to meet the standard of care for her condition. Failing to provide adequate treatment for a detainee with a life-threatening illness is not only inhumane, it is negligent and reckless," Ansari wrote in a letter to ICE's acting director, Todd Lyons.[7] I spoke to Ansari about her visit with Yari, and she told me of the critical importance of "members of Congress all across the country to continue going to the detention centers." Some members of Congress were charged with crimes for attempting to conduct oversight visits.[8]

Before the oversight and inspection systems were dismantled, Laura St. John, managing attorney of the Florence Immigrant and Refugee Rights Project, tells me that oversight wasn't enough: "Because ultimately, oversight with no power to enforce—that's very little oversight at all."

Now, with even less oversight, what happens? How can we reckon with what people experience inside to put a stop to it—and hold people accountable for the harm that has already been done? We have firsthand accounts that, if in varying degrees and ways, the camp is consistently dehumanizing and torturous, and sometimes deadly. Or, as one formerly detained person told me, when you're in the camps . . .

"You're Like the Dead"

Paul (a pseudonym) is a 34-year-old migrant from Rwanda. He has high cheekbones and a worry-wrinkled forehead. When I met with him in the summer of 2023, he was slouching in his chair, wearing jeans, a baseball hat, and a T-shirt that read "The love in the air is thicker than smoke."

Paul was born just a few years before the beginning of the Rwandan genocide, in which Hutu militias killed nearly 80 percent of the country's population of another ethnic group, the Tutsis. Estimates put the Tutsi death toll, in just about a hundred days, at nearly a million. Like many people in the country at that time, Paul witnessed extraordinary horrors; he told me that six of his siblings and both of his parents were killed in the violence.

As an adolescent, he escaped to the Republic of Congo, living in an orphanage there before ending up on the streets. With the help of his sister, he was accepted to the United States as a refugee in 2015 at age twenty-four.

In the US, Paul had a lot of trouble adjusting. Struggling with culture shock and a language barrier, he dealt with anxiety, depression, and suicidality associated with post-traumatic stress disorder. After a criminal conviction, he was put in removal proceedings and was sent to the Eloy immigration camp in October 2022.

Paul described the conditions in the camp as worse than those he had faced during a stint in a Yuma prison. Feeling deeply depressed, he got into an altercation with another person there and was eventually placed on suicide watch—which is often experienced as a form of punishment. "I was very alone," he told me. "I asked why they couldn't take me to where the other people were." No answer came.

Of conditions on suicide watch, Paul said, "It takes your life and puts it at the very bottom. It got to a point where you're kind of not living." It was so bad inside, he reflected, that he considered whether it might be better to face again the horrors and fears he had fled in Rwanda. That was when, Paul told me, he felt "like the dead."

Isolation—a detention tactic that captures the naked intentions of the camp—seeks to reduce a person to less than one: to break a person from their human ties, to break them from who they are. The United Nations considers solitary confinement "prolonged" if it lasts fifteen days. It also classifies prolonged solitary confinement as torture. Over a span of just fourteen months, from April 2024 to May 2025, more than 10,500 people were held in solitary confinement in immigration camps across the United States. On average, they spent thirty-eight days alone in their cages.[9] As one trans woman, Kaysi, who spent various stints in solitary in a New Mexico camp told me, "It's killing me." That, and 108,000 other forms of torture and cruelty, is what it looks like when the camp is winning. It also reminds us what will ultimately break the camp: unity in resistance.

Nora Ahmed, director of ACLU Louisiana, tells me that she commonly sees people locked in camps reach a breaking point after about three and a half months inside, at which point they start thinking, "I can't do this anymore, because I'm either going to die here or I'm going to die elsewhere." It is often the unknown, Ahmed explains, that tips someone over the edge. People in prisons have been sentenced and know, at least, what their maximum term will be. In immigration camps, however, someone's time spent inside is discretionary: ICE *could* release them. They could also hold them, even during appeal, for as long as it takes to find a place to deport them to. That sentence can become indefinite.

With immigration camps, Ahmed adds,

> it's terrifying because they could just keep you there day in and day out. . . . They could deport you to a country that you've never been to in your entire life. You could end up in prison in that country; you could end up killed in that country; you could end up back in the very country that you left because you were being persecuted there.

With the help of a team of attorneys from the Florence Project, Paul finally won his release. The camp, however, continued to haunt him.

The Hidden Cost

In 2025, Jim Recht, a Harvard psychiatrist who works with Physicians for Human Rights (PHR), traveled to Panama to interview non-Panamanian migrants who had been deported there from the US. Recht's assessment was stark: He tells me he found people who had suffered "very significant psychological abuse."

Recht had been contracted by PHR after a group of more than a hundred migrants were detained in January at the Otay Mesa camp in San Diego. For over a week, the migrants were held in overcrowded, windowless cells before being forced—without warning—onto military aircraft. Their phones and documents were confiscated, and they were deported to Panama City without ever being given the chance to request asylum. Once in Panama, they were shuffled between hotels and a remote facility in the Darién jungle that had once been a prison. "The conditions were horrific," Recht says. "No physical violence, but extreme deprivation—bad food, suffocating heat, and an utter sense of powerlessness."

Recht and his team met with two dozen of the deportees in a Catholic Charities shelter in Panama City, where the doctors conducted medical and psychological evaluations, documenting what they called "acute stress disorder" and "layered trauma." Nearly everyone, Recht notes, displayed one symptom rarely discussed but of immense consequence: a total collapse of sleep. "Sleep is the thing," he tells me. "It's almost universal—the inability to rest. People are haunted at night by the guards' laughter, by the fear that they'll be taken again. Their dreams become terrifying reenactments of what they've survived." Once sleeplessness sets in, he explains, "resilience deteriorates and people become vulnerable to obsessive anxiety, guilt, and despair."

One of the women Recht evaluated, Alice, a 27-year-old Iranian who fled persecution for protesting the hijab law, was separated from her brother at the US border and secretly deported to Panama. When Recht interviewed her, she was waking nightly from dreams that she was again on a military plane being sent back to Iran. Beatrice, a 26-year-old from Eritrea, described watching one person in a US camp collapse during an asthma attack as guards dragged her across the floor. She, too, began suffering relentless nightmares and said she sometimes thought of ending her life.

The psychic misery of detention, Recht explains, doesn't end when the walls disappear. It follows people. The destruction of sleep, the dread, the loss of basic trust in society: the architecture of the camp reconstructed inside the mind.

Recht also evaluated Barry, a 36-year-old father from Iran who had fled with his wife and children after being imprisoned and beaten for attending a peaceful protest in Tehran. When Border Patrol agents apprehended them near San Diego, Barry was never provided an interpreter or a chance to explain his fear of persecution. Guards mocked him, calling him "Arab," and within days, he and his family were handcuffed, shackled, and loaded onto a military plane. When they awoke, they were in Panama—a country none of them had ever been to, where they were again confined and forbidden to communicate freely. Transferred from one camp to another, Barry began to lose his grasp on where safety might exist.

In Panama, Barry developed severe insomnia. After several nights of near-total sleeplessness, he began experiencing waking dreams—momentary dozes that collapsed into nightmares in which he was back in Iran, being arrested again. Even after being released and moving, temporarily, to Panama City, the sleeplessness persisted. His body began to show signs of the psychological strain: tremors, accompanied by a constant mental static that made it hard for him to focus. He developed a stutter, which he had never had before. "When you destroy a person's sleep," Recht explains, "you destroy their ability to heal." Sleep is the mind's reset. Without it, trauma consolidates rather than dissolves. People become trapped.

In detention, the destruction of rest—through noise, light, fear, and constant surveillance—is deliberate and structural. Your sense of time fractures, your emotions spiral, and your body loses its ability to regulate stress. As a 2025 *Guardian* article reveals, this sleep denial is not only pervasive but physically built into the camp system. At one facility, detainees described fluorescent lights running twenty-four hours a day, occluded windows, and such negligible contrast between the hours that those inside "couldn't tell if it was day or night." The report explains that the resulting disruption of circadian rhythms is linked to serious health conditions and that the lighting conditions may amount to torture.[10]

One global study of immigration detention confirmed that though many migrants came into the situation with preexisting traumas, detention both exacerbated extant symptoms and was itself an independent variable that increased the likelihood of mental illness.[11]

You can close the gates, you can move people to another country, but the camp, as experienced by Paul, Barry, and so many others, can keep living within.

The Toll on the Community

Drive into Eloy, Arizona, where Paul was held, and you will see a city whose economy has been strangled by cages. The desert town, whose population hovers around twenty thousand, is home to three privately run state prisons and one of the nation's largest immigration camps. For years, Eloy has acted as a pass-through signatory: It holds the intergovernmental service agreement with ICE, then subcontracts operations out to CoreCivic for camps, including the Dilley, Texas, family camp discussed earlier.* On paper, Eloy is the "partner." In reality, it's a fig leaf. When people detained in camps suffer and die—as they have, at alarming rates—the city claims it has no oversight, no liability. When beds go empty, though, ICE keeps paying, and Eloy keeps collecting a fee.

The financial receipts are telling. ICE contracts almost always include the aforementioned "guaranteed minimums," which means the government pays for a set number of beds regardless of whether they're filled. A Government Accountability Office study showed that in 2020, nationwide, contract utilization often hovered around 75 percent, meaning a quarter of the detention system was ghost capacity and that ICE "spent millions of dollars a month on unused detention space"—funded by taxpayers, enriching private operators, and depleting resources that could be deployed for the needs of communities.[12]

This is the first paradox of detention economics: The community hosting the cages rarely has control over what

* The city also contracts out with the Hawaii Department of Corrections, allowing CoreCivic to make money off of locking up people imprisoned from the island state.

happens inside them, but it almost always pays a price. That price includes the fallout from the suffering within the camps, including the frequent use of emergency medical services.

Communities are often sold detention centers as a form of rural revitalization. Politicians and corporate reps show up with PowerPoints promising stable jobs, new tax revenue, an economic shot in the arm. The reality is more fragile. A major 2023 report by Innovation Law Lab found that detention does not deliver long-term economic development. Instead, towns risk dependency on a single, politically volatile revenue stream. Economists studying prison towns have long shown similar patterns: short-term job bumps followed by stagnation, outmigration, and persistent poverty. As the authors of the report conclude, "Prisons produce fewer jobs than would other industries as they rely on incarcerated people to perform largely unpaid labor instead of hiring from the local community."[13] Instead of lifting up communities, investment in camps entrenches precarity.

When it comes to building and operating a camp, the profiteers typically seek to do business with the lowest bidder. Generally, this means local businesses can't compete with large national corporations. Thus, when a camp is constructed, the main beneficiaries are out-of-town construction companies that typically employ their own engineering, design, and construction personnel rather than turning to the local workforce. Likewise, camps and prisons alike usually send capital outside of local economies to procure linens, food, medicine, maintenance supplies, heavy equipment, and other items necessary to the running of a prison. In fact, rather than supporting local businesses, camp construction is associated with the shuttering of local businesses and proliferation of big box stores.[14] In Tehachapi, California—a town of roughly twelve thousand that housed two state prisons during the 1990s—741 local businesses failed over the course of a decade, while retail and fast-food chains took over the local market.[15] Compared to prison towns, nonprison towns have a greater rate of growth in the number of new businesses, nonagricultural employment, average household wages, retail sales, median value of owner occupied housing, and total number of new housing units.[16] As Ian Philabaum of Innovation Law Lab tells me, "When a prison moves into your town, that's a sign that your town is at a dead end."

The logic of the camp seeps into everything: those who are detained, the surrounding town, and the people—guards, managers, healthcare workers, attorneys, and others who work inside them. The emotional and physical—and surely spiritual—impact on guards is hard to overstate. Their workplaces are large, prefab-looking buildings surrounded by razor wire, divided into cells and barracks, mostly devoid of natural light, frequently infested with mold, bugs, or rats. Staff are expected to exert domination over large numbers of people, discipline detained individuals, respond to emergencies, and frequently work double shifts. People working under such circumstances suffer.

Studies of prison workers consistently demonstrate that they have high stress and burnout levels. Researchers have also found that, compared to workers in other settings, prison workers experience increased levels of physical and mental illness. According to a study from an organization focused on the mental health of correctional officers, 31 percent of corrections officers report serious psychological stress—more than three times the rate of the general population—and 34 percent experience PTSD symptoms, surpassing rates among combat veterans.[17]

The deleterious economic impact seeps beyond municipal budgets: Detention centers also drain public health resources. A Vera Institute report, published in 2020 at the height of the COVID-19 pandemic, modeled how outbreaks inside detention centers bled into surrounding towns.[18] Around the same time, I reported for *The Intercept* that, as of August of that year, about 5.5 percent of COVID cases in the entire country were attributable to spread from immigration detention centers.[19] Rural counties with detention centers saw higher COVID caseloads, seeded from poorly controlled facilities. The boundary between "inside" and "outside" of these camps was porous: Staff went home to their families; contractors moved between jobs; sick detainees were left to languish, unable to socially distance and not always provided with masks or given the chance to wash their hands. Further, in the early days of the pandemic, the US deported hundreds of people infected with the virus, including to countries like Guatemala and Haiti, prompting outbreaks in countries with less developed healthcare systems.[20]

It isn't just viruses. A 2022 peer-reviewed study traced hospitalizations in Texas directly to nearby detention facilities.[21] ICE's own medical subdivision, the ICE Health Service Corp, contracts out complex care, burdening the hospitals nearest the camps. Reimbursement, however, is slow and partial, and county hospitals are left holding the bag.

In 2025, *Wired* obtained 911 call logs from ten of the largest camps in the country. Hundreds of distress calls came from those facilities in a single year, many for seizures, suicide attempts, chest pains, and pregnancy complications. The costs—overtime pay, equipment—were externalized onto towns that had never voted for cages but now lived under their weight. According to the article, "Dispatch data from 911 calls reveal how quickly medical emergencies can spiral inside these remote, crowded facilities—places where urgent care delivery is already often delayed, falls on overworked staff, or is hindered by 'insufficient or malfunctioning' equipment."[22]

Even when residents aren't directly employed by or servicing detention centers, the presence of cages warps community life. Criminologist Yael Jácome has documented how immigration enforcement depresses crime reporting, especially among Latino residents.[23] When ICE is visible, when deportation feels proximate, community trust erodes. Police are rightly feared. Schools see absenteeism rise. People retreat from public space.

In 2025 I spoke with a group of social workers in Tucson, Arizona, who had begun offering emotional support to families impacted by immigration enforcement.[24] One woman, Yarlidis, whose husband had been arrested at a local hospital and then swiftly deported, was so traumatized and fearful she wouldn't let her two teenage daughters attend school for months. She described to me a prolonged state of panic that ultimately prompted a decision to self-deport. "I didn't want to see my children in handcuffs," Yarlidis said. The day before they turned themselves in at an ICE office, Yarlidis's nine-year-old daughter, Emily, who feared being disappeared, brainstormed with her mom where they were going to hide bluetooth GPS trackers so the social workers could try to track their whereabouts. "Because if they don't know where we are, something bad might happen," Emily said. Early the next morning, the family prepared to submit themselves to ICE outside one of the field offices as community members stood by in support. I was also present, reporting on their story. I watched as Emily struggled to let go of her home. She latched onto her grandmother and some friends who were tearfully seeing her off. As she walked toward the barred door, she stopped to give me a tight hug. Not knowing what to say, I told her to take care of her mom. She promised she would.

This chilling effect on individuals, families, communities is pervasive. In detention towns, the constant reminder—the barbed wire on the drive to school, the busloads of shackled migrants at the gas station, the Border Patrol checkpoints when heading to the grocery store—seeps into civic life. Detention not only captures the detained but can drown the community itself in an atmosphere of fear.

The Costs of Dependency

There's also a more subtle but corrosive impact: political capture. When a city budget depends on detention dollars, officials begin defending the cages more than their constituents. They lobby for contract renewals. They paint local opponents as threatening jobs. And they normalize what should be unthinkable: profiting off of human caging.

Louisiana offers a cautionary tale. Dozens of the state's rural parishes rely on ICE per diem payments, where sheriffs have admitted that without immigrant detainees, their budgets would collapse. Jackson Parish, for one, receives seventy-four dollars a day for each migrant locked up, or about three times what the state pays to house someone convicted of a crime.[25] Such dependency bends the political landscape, turning local lawmen into de facto wardens for federal detention and deportation policy. Indeed, when communities start measuring prosperity by the number of detention beds, resistance to closure hardens.

The lesson from years of study is stark: Immigration camps and prisons are not anchors of prosperity but fiscal sandbags dragging down towns. They hollow out economies, sap public health, and contort local politics. As a spokesperson for Arizona Governor Katie Hobbs told me after the state sold an abandoned prison, for $15 million, to a for-profit contractor that works with ICE: "The administration had a choice: either keep wasting taxpayer dollars maintaining a building the state wasn't using, or sell it for money that can be used to expand access to affordable child care, invest in public education and fight veterans' homelessness." Pressed, the spokesperson said, "There were three bidders for the facility, and the state sold it to the highest bidder." In other words, the state decided to fund childcare and veteran healthcare by locking up migrants.

Breaking the Spell

Detention is often justified as a national security necessity, an abstract policy that nonetheless plays out and inflicts harms that are local, lived, and measurable. Those harms impact the guard who says the job working in a camp "hurts [their] soul."[26] They impact the county treasurer who watches per diem payments vanish into corporate accounts while schools clamor for funding.*[27] They impact the kids in Louisiana

* The town of Eloy makes twenty-five cents a day per person detained, while ICE pays private contractors, such as CoreCivic,

who grow up recognizing that cages are their county's main industry.

When you strip away the rhetoric, detention looks less like an economic engine and more like a scam. Corporations profit. ICE bureaucrats hit their bed quotas, but towns are left with the fallout: sick detainees, strained services, and poisoned politics.

Closing camps is first and foremost about freeing those currently locked inside—and anyone who fears being caged in one. It is also about freeing communities from a predatory system that siphons their wealth, corrodes their politics, and endangers their health. To close a camp is to open a horizon—for migrants and also for towns conscripted into the machinery of detention. In closing the camps, we have room to—are indeed forced to—imagine other ways of building community.

---

up to $165 dollars a day per person detained. Elizabeth Trovall, "Who Profits from a $45 Billion Investment in Immigrant Detention?," *Marketplace*, August 18, 2025, https://www.marketplace.org/story/2025/08/18/who-profits-from-detaining-immigrants.

3

"YOU SHALL DO A BAD JOB FOR THE GERMANS"

"You shall protect anyone chased by the Germans."

So reads one of the Danish "Ten Commandments" of resistance. As part of the Nazis' blitzkrieg through Europe, their army invaded Denmark in 1940, taking over the country in just a few hours. And though the invaders met no military pushback, regular Danes organized other forms of resistance, showing that even where a traditional military standoff was unwinnable, creative sabotage had its place. The Danes staged worker slowdowns and two-minute work stoppages. They marched and sang resistance songs. And they distributed a list of commandments, including the above—*protect anyone chased by the Germans*—and:

- You shall do a bad job for the Germans.
- You shall work slowly for the Germans.
- You shall destroy important machines and tools.
- You shall destroy everything which may be of benefit to the Germans.[1]

The anti-Nazi credo was an example of *samfundssind*, or "community-mindedness," a term invoked during the Danish resistance last century, as well as reemerging as part of community-resilience and mutual aid projects during the COVID pandemic. As Sarah Sophie Flicker observes in a *Nation* essay on Danish solidarity movements' "more muted history of defiance during WWII," pushback doesn't have to be big and loud or escalatory. "I learned," she writes, "that the Danish resistance didn't arrive all at once. Like what we are witnessing now in the United States, it unfolded gradually—slow, then more quickly, then full tilt—driven by flash points that demanded escalation and deepened solidarity."[2]

People have been resisting detention camps in the United States—through variations of *samfundssind* and other means—since the Chinese Six organized mass resistance efforts in the nineteenth century and individuals refused to carry papers, subjected themselves to arrest, wrote poems about their detention, and kept crossing borders.

Today, the American spirit of community resilience manifests in neighborhood ICE watches, rapid response and mutual aid networks, legal organizations and NGOs, as well as both organized and spontaneous moments of refusal and solidarity in the streets as our neighbors, family members, and colleagues are surveilled, targeted, kidnapped, and arrested. Almost any act against the camp is worth the effort: blowing a whistle to alert your neighbors, holding up your phone to record video of ICE activity, calling your congressperson, insisting on your basic rights, using your body to block a kidnapper's van, or forging closer ties with your community. Immigration scholar Michelle Castañeda writes movingly of "kinesthetic empathy," observing how accompaniment, or simply being with people who are targeted (especially in vulnerable situations), can be a radical act.[3] It can be a functional one, too.

In September 2025, a close friend of mine in Chicago's heavily targeted and seriously organized Rogers Park neighborhood was heading out to do a quick errand when he heard the first whistle. As he took his own whistle out of his pocket, and more neighbors started blowing theirs, a man on a bicycle rushed quickly by him. My friend approached the scene: Border Patrol agents in a luxury, window-tinted SUV were blocking a woman's car. The man who had rushed by was using his bike like a bullfighter's muleta, holding it sideways and yelling at the agents. Five of them spilled out of their SUV, one of them wielding a telescoping nightstick, another aiming a taser. They cornered the man against the fence. The alley filled with more whistles and a woman's blood-curdling scream from her window: "Get the fuck out of my neighborhood!" As the agents were occupied with the man, the woman in the car who had been the initial target drove off. Soon other neighbors came out of their houses, filming on their phones, flipping the script. One woman stood next to the man being cornered and held up her phone at the agents. The act of filming seemed to have as much power, for a moment, as the threat of violence from the agent's nightstick. After a tense standoff, the agents jumped back in their SUV and drove off. No arrests were made. My friend made sure to get their license plate number.

"If we want to accompany another person, it is not enough to advocate for them from a safe distance," Castañeda writes. "Accompaniment means inhabiting the spaces they inhabit, which are generally spaces of struggle, danger, or isolation."[4]

But mere presence *can* also make a difference. In immigration court, if you're represented by an attorney, you're fifteen times more likely to be able to stay in the country lawfully than you would be without one.[5] Any form of kinesthetic empathy—you don't need to be a lawyer—can protect and shift the way the state treats someone they view as unwanted.

As community organizer and scholar Juan Ortiz, cofounder of El Paso's Casa Carmelita, tells me, "Come to assist, come to resist, but don't come to witness." All are welcome, but by *all*, Juan means: all who are willing to be productive. In 2018 and 2019, Juan was on the front lines of community-led efforts to push back against a camp imprisoning children in Tornillo, Texas—many of whom were ripped away from their parents as part of the family-separation strategy—and has long organized to offer basic food and aid to migrants, as well as to push the abuses of ICE and Border Patrol into public consciousness. In 2019 he sounded the alarm, for example, to the plight of hundreds of migrants corralled by Border Patrol into an outdoor holding pen under a bridge in El Paso. Juan grew up on the border and, from a tender age, was targeted—marginalized, scapegoated, and criminalized—along with many of his family members and neighbors.

"I come from real not-fucking-around roots," Ortiz tells me, which is partly why he pushes allies and advocates to take concrete steps. "Efficacy matters, you need a result, you need something tangible." His focus is action, "not voyeuristic witnessing."

"Come do some shit, don't just stare," Ortiz says. "Do some shit" means fighting detention in coalition on the streets and town councils and state legislatures, as well as building toward a positive post-detention society.

He explains why "anti-detention work has to be central." Detention is a keystone in the government's capacity to target and deport, to break up communities, he says. All of the pomp and terror in the streets during Trump's second administration—the prowling agents in military gear, the mass arrests, the stalking of schools and courtrooms—depends on the government having somewhere to detain the people they arrest. The camp is the linchpin of immigration enforcement.

The criminalization of migrants "touches at the heart and soul of liberalism," Ortiz says. "Once people get on board with calling other people criminals, it all becomes one amalgamation that liberals wholeheartedly agree with." That's how the concept of "border security" has taken priority over human security or human dignity in mainstream discourse over the last few decades. What border security looks like in 2026 is not only ICE and Border Patrol wreaking havoc on our communities, but the agencies increasingly taking on the characteristics of a secret police force.[6]

The urgency, Juan and others argue, cannot be overstated. At the same time, he and others counsel, we must also be calculated, not merely reactive. This is why learning from veterans in the fight is so critical.

Play the Long Game

Fred Tsao, senior policy counsel for Illinois Coalition for Immigrant and Refugee Rights, has been fighting immigration camps for two decades. He's built up quite the record: stopping at least nine camps from going operational in the

Midwest, as well as pushing the state of Illinois to pass the Illinois Way Forward Act, signed into law in 2021, which prohibits the state and local governments from engaging in federal immigration enforcement.* It is the states that arguably have the most power to push back against the camps, and Illinois led the way, followed by California, Oregon, Washington, New Jersey, and a few others.

Before the Way Forward Act was passed, county jails across Illinois could contract with federal immigration authorities: Jails received payment from ICE in exchange for keeping immigrants detained while they awaited their hearings in immigration court. These agreements, which collectively earned county jails as much as $10 million annually, extended the reach of federal immigration enforcement into local governments and terrorized resident immigrants, their families, and their communities.[7] Then Tsao and others started shutting down the camps.

"We're a relatively liberated territory," Tsao told me of Illinois. We spoke just weeks before ICE, along with Border Patrol and the National Guard, started circling Chicago in 2025 as part of Operation "Midway Blitz"—before they came outfitted for an invasion and landed helicopters on buildings, shot at bystanders, body-slammed protesters, tear-gassed local police, dragged teachers out of preschools,

---

* As the Immigrant Legal Resource Center notes, "Over the last decade, 70–75 percent of ICE arrests in the interior of the US have been handoffs from another law enforcement agency, be it a local or state jail or federal prison." "State Map on Immigration Enforcement 2024," Immigrant Legal Resource Center, https://www.ilrc.org/state-map-immigration-enforcement-2024.

and made a militaristic show of patrolling the Chicago River. Still, despite the martial circus staged in and around the city, ICE was limited by their capacity to cage the people they were arresting. That's in large part thanks to Tsao and the community coalitions he's been working with.

The son of two immigrants, Tsao explained why he's been in the fight for so long. "My father was detained [decades ago] at the ICE building in San Francisco," he told me. "We suspect there was some chicanery in his getting approved and released, but he was finally able to fix his status." A delayed part of the Chinese Confession Program—an initiative of the Immigration and Naturalization Service rolled out in the late 1950s that allowed Chinese migrants who had entered the US without authorization to "confess" their status and be "legalized"—Tsao's father got what Tsao called a mini-amnesty. "I strongly believe so many other people are just as deserving as my dad," Tsao told me. "[They] deserve the chance to raise a family, pursue dreams, live a decent life here in this country."

Tsao believes we'll get through this moment, "but a lot of damage is going to happen in the meantime." He counseled that the current strategy should be to minimize the damage and empower each other, which he suggested we can do in a number of ways: by preparing ourselves, knowing and fighting for our rights, defending our neighbors, and playing the long game—namely, stopping more camps from being built. Part of this empowerment also comes from learning the history of resistance.

Tsao pointed to the example of Elkhart County in northeastern Indiana, which in 2017 and 2018 was facing down a $100 million, 1,200-bed immigration camp, to be run by CoreCivic.[8] Elkhart has a local college and a sizable Latino population, Tsao said, which gave the organizers the idea to mobilize students, Latinos, and local businesses to push back. Despite the county voting overwhelmingly for Donald Trump in 2016, the community soon rallied against the camp. A turning point came with their success in harnessing business interests, as illustrated when a spokesperson for a major regional employer, Elkhart Plastics, said, "Putting an ICE facility here would hamper our abilities to attract people." In turn, the organizers convinced CoreCivic to back out: "We have been assessing whether the Elkhart community would be a good fit for this project," a spokesman for CoreCivic told *The Wall Street Journal*.[9] They never came back. Efforts to become unappealing to camp corporations, even by merely showing that there will be a fight, can—sometimes—make a difference.

While not all site fights are as relatively easy as the one in Elkhart, Tsao said, "There's a playbook." It usually starts with research: who's for it, who are potential allies against. "You need to do a power analysis," he said. "What are the potential obstacles? Are there environmental issues? Could there be litigation? There may be local legislation, resolutions, other ways to throw sand in the gears, can we deny roadway easements?" Local elections are also a point of potential leverage. For instance, the town of Joliet, Illinois, was the site of a planned detention center in 2021, but threats of primarying a city council member who was provisionally in support of the camp helped fend it off.

"Another really effective tool is the yard sign," Tsao said, holding up an old sign as he spoke to me from his office: "Crete Detention Center," the sign read, with a big X through the words. "One weirdo putting a yard sign in their front yard or window, two people, who knows. But if you start peppering a small town or subdivision, people are going to start paying attention."

Tsao acknowledged that since his string of victories, the landscape has changed: ICE has significantly more money and is backed by an administration hellbent on building new facilities, even in the face of fierce local pushback. "It's not so much a change in playbook," he said, "but that we need creativity. We need to find more effective ways to rally the opposition."

Part of that means offering a positive vision for what's possible, not just critiques of the camp. "Can community be rebuilt in a way that benefits people?" Tsao asked, adding, "All we're seeing right now is destruction."

The moral question may seem difficult to harness, but the local approach, even hyperlocal, can be effective: How do you want to treat your neighbor? Do you want your kids to grow up in the shadow of suffering that comes with a camp? A good exercise for allies, even veterans in the fight, can be a simple act of empathy: put yourself in the shoes of the person targeted or locked into a camp.

No One Deserves the Camp

Besides Tsao, there are few people more experienced, and with more clarity on the history and current needs of the movement, than Silky Shah, the executive director of Detention Watch Network. "Having worked on this for twenty years, this is worse than I could have actually imagined," Shah tells me of the reality in 2026.

In today's rapid expansion of the camp system, she sees continuities with the history of detention, as well as new challenges. "Detention has long been a very clear space where people are stripped of their rights," she says, explaining that while recent cases are clearly alarming—people being arrested without warrants, green card holders being picked up—none of this is new. But targeting people for speech, such as Mahmoud Khalil—a Columbia University graduate student arrested and detained for his pro-Palestine stance—is, she believes, a "departure." "This is where I see something that portends."

Shah warns against falling into the trap of "innocence frameworks," which accept that while *some* people do not deserve the camp or shouldn't suffer, others should. As we saw in chapter 1, immigrants (Chinese, Mexican, Japanese, Haitian, and others) were criminalized explicitly because of their race, or as a form of labor arbitrage, as part of a broader push toward incarceration. Innocence frameworks "reinforce the idea that immigration enforcement is about public safety," Shah says, when it's actually about labor and racial control. When we argue against the camp by focusing on the innocence of the people inside, making arguments like "'Oh, this person didn't do anything wrong,'" Shah explains, "it accepts that public safety is the central thing to consider when it comes to immigration."

That's a problem, she observes, not only because it throws some people under the bus but because it misses the chance for systemic change. "One of our biggest challenges in the movement is when you have so many lawyers focusing on the individual and the thing that's going to help that individual." That framing, according to Shah, pushes people to come up with emergency or individually specific "solutions" like alternatives to detention (often in the form of ankle bracelet surveillance) or marginal improvements to camp conditions. Those efforts have led to both an entrenchment and expansion of the system.

Consider the push by advocates in the late aughts for the use of prosecutorial discretion—a true individualization of immigration reform—in which judges or deportation officers could deprioritize particular cases and let someone remain in the country. While around seventy-five thousand people were protected from deportation through prosecutorial discretion under the Obama administration, the total number of people arrested, detained, and deported continued to rise.[10] The federal government, while offering visible humanitarian protection to some, was also ramping up its prosecution of people for crossing the border.* "At the same time that the Obama administration was supposedly providing more discretion for deprioritizing some deportations, it was simultaneously increasing the criminalization that would make it harder for many immigrants to get relief," writes Shah in *Unbuild Walls*.[11] That individualization of protections can function as a weapon—targeting and dismantling collective efforts that have the capacity for more broadly focused, systemic changes.

Rejecting "carceral humanism"—as softening the edges of cages is sometimes called—is a crucial political and moral step. The solution, Shah argues, is not better food, more counselors, or access to lawyers; it's tearing down the walls.

---

* In 2011, more people were prosecuted for illegal reentry into the country than for any other federal charge. In 2001, there were just over eight thousand prosecutions for illegal reentry; ten years later, under Obama, there were over thirty-seven thousand such prosecutions. Transactional Records Access Clearinghouse, "Illegal Reentry Becomes Top Criminal Charge," Syracuse University, 2011.

The demand for closure rather than improvement recognizes that detention is not broken but operating as it was designed: to punish, isolate, and deter. If the ultimate goal is freedom, then the horizon must be abolition. Anything less risks building more tolerable camps, rather than a society without them. For immigration detention, that means closure—not reform—is the only true victory.

While the current moment has its obvious dangers and challenges, Shah knows that any time the system is in such flux, it also opens opportunities. It's a reminder to people that, in her words, "this isn't how we've always done things. This isn't how we always have to do things."

Taking advantage of these opportunities means bringing more people into the movement. "Find the people in your community who are doing this work and connect with them and figure out how you can support," Shah counsels. "It could be five hours a month. It doesn't have to be a lot of your time. It's [about] trying to figure out the role you can play. What is the thing that you can offer?"

As Shah points out, "Finding your people is a really big part of staying in the work"—a dimension amply illustrated by the experience of Marcela Hernandez, another organizer at Detention Watch Network. She has been fighting detention and deportation for twenty years, ever since her uncle was arrested and deported from California when she was in college. His deportation left two young kids without a present father. "Growing up undocumented, with police stopping us and reporting us to ICE—I wanted to do something about it," she tells me.

Hernandez moved to Chicago after college, cutting her teeth with local organizations there. Our conversation takes place as she plans an imminent convening of more than 120 people involved in anti-detention work. Their stated goal: "to take a step back and think about how we're fighting against the system expanding, not only in the next three years, but beyond." That fight begins locally.

"Mutual aid organizations are going to be the building blocks for future organizing," Hernandez explains. Mutual aid, what author Dean Spade also calls "survival work," is the power that comes from finding your people.[12] These connections, that community network, is the grassroots base of building something better than a camp. "Mutual aid work has sometimes been perceived as less important than work to try to stop the systems, but the reality is that all effective resistance movements do both: attack the systems of domination and support the people who are in crisis because of them," Spade tells me. That crisis, however, can be overlooked—especially when the online attention economy can hopscotch us from crisis to inanity to crisis with the flick of a thumb.

Hernandez says a lot of the work, especially with directly impacted folks, is "to paint the picture of harm that detention and deportation is putting on communities."

"A lot of us who get involved with organizing, the first entry may be signing a petition, showing up to a protest, joining an Instagram live or webinar." These are all good entry points, she observes, but "for folks directly impacted, the stakes are higher. If they don't fight back, they risk family separation, being deported to their death."

"Train Up"

To fight back, it is not enough just to have community; we must have a trained, focused, community. On June 6, 2025, what began as an ordinary workday for garment workers at Ambiance—a women's fast-fashion company in downtown Los Angeles—turned into terror. ICE raided both the retail store and its warehouse headquarters, arresting fourteen people, with witnesses describing "unlawful mass collateral arrests." Families say their loved ones were taken without due process, without access to attorneys, and without regard for their rights.

Alejo (who asked for me to use only her first name) works at Trabajadores Unidos Workers United in San Francisco and got a call that same day from her mother: "They got your uncle." A little while later she got another call: It was actually two of her uncles. In total, ICE had abducted fourteen members of the extended Zapotec community.

Marcela Hernandez emphasizes the impact of the fear such crackdowns incite. People may be afraid to go to work, or to be on the streets. "Folks can resort to isolating themselves in their homes," she says. And if people don't have connections with each other, it's really hard to know where and when their family members were taken.

The intention of raids like these is to isolate and terrify, Hernandez explains. But in Los Angeles, that terror was quickly met with resistance. The day after the raid, Alejo was already down in LA with other families of people who had been kidnapped—a group of over sixty people who had showed up that first morning. They spent two full days focusing on gathering information, processing, and planning. Alejo and some of the others began training people to speak out, offering them practice talking into microphones, making posters, leaning into their Indigenous culture and roots. Out of this urgency, the campaign Lucha Zapoteca was born—a collective named in honor of the detained workers' Indigenous Zapotec identity. That was all taking place in the first weeks of the federal crackdown in Los Angeles. "We were organizing and there were literally helicopters flying over our heads," Alejo says. The group had mixed status, and yet, despite roaming ICE and Border Patrol agents, they decided to stage the first protest at the same factory where the raid had taken place. "We were facing a very violent and aggressive administration," Alejo recalls. "We were facing a deportation machine. It was going to be really hard to take this on, but not impossible."

"We're really good at rapid response, at blocking busses, things like that," Alejo reflects. "But what can I do when someone is already detained? I didn't know. I could only share what I thought was possible." She explains how she and others learned how the bond process worked (issuing a financial guarantee to the government) in order to legally break people out of the camps. When the Trump administration effectively canceled bond, the crew pivoted to learn how to use habeas petitions—essentially forcing the court to review whether there is lawful basis for an individual's detention. They were training themselves to navigate the tangled web of immigration law.

Within weeks, the families, alongside organizers and allies—collaborating with groups like the California Collaborative for Immigrant Justice—had secured legal representation for the people who were abducted. Through their organizing, they learned that the workers had been taken to the Adelanto camp, an hour and a half from Los Angeles.

Organizers raised tens of thousands of dollars in mutual aid funds to sustain the workers' families, suddenly bereft of income. By late June, they had won their first major victory: The first of the detained workers was released.

Lucha Zapoteca began hosting gatherings where neighbors reaffirmed their commitment to the collective struggle. Leadership development became central: Families kept pushing for habeas hearings, gathering letters of support, and power-mapping local decision-makers, which I discuss below in chapter 4. By November, though two of the original fourteen had been deported, Lucha Zapoteca had secured the release of most of the others.

They've since developed an Anti-Deportation Organizing Committee, or ADOC. Alejo describes the importance not just of doing defensive mutual aid on the streets, such as establishing ICE-watch networks, but of conducting anti-deportation legal trainings. "We need more spaces that make place for leadership development to take these skills and talk to other people," she says. "We need to train up."

The fight for those arrested in the Ambiance raid is ongoing. While a few remain in detention—facing the grinding violence of the immigration system—their families are no longer isolated. They are organizers, advocates, and leaders in a growing coalition connecting a hyperlocal struggle to broader campaigns.

Training and popular education play a crucial role in the fight, Hernandez emphasizes. Organizers resisting ICE must continually ask, "How are we building power to really change the system? How are we being mindful that we're not recreating the system but actually chipping away at the prison industrial complex?"

Speaking in late 2025, she says that things are happening so quickly, and under such shocking conditions, it's hard to keep thinking about long-term change. "At the end of the day it comes back to organizing," she says. "If folks are organized on their block, if folks are fighting back, if folks have a vision to invest in the needs of communities, they can build real and lasting power and stop investing in agencies harming us and separating families."

This means thinking hard about budgets, and how budgets affect community values. While that may seem like technical, boring, or daunting work, you can begin by simply asking, "What else do you want in your community? What other kinds of jobs are good for the land, good for the community? How do we move away from a carceral economy to a more regenerative economy?" Hernandez offers examples of a community clinic, a garden, or a hospital—"things that are nourishing the community."

Marysville, California—a small rural town a couple hours northeast of San Francisco—provides an illustrative example. The local jail had been leasing out 150 beds, at $150 per day, to ICE. The suffering inside prompted a fierce and creative campaign to end the ICE contract. Laura Duarte Bateman, one of the essential organizers, shared with me a long list of what community members wanted instead of an ICE camp. Their ideas included "an organization that could help correctional officers find other jobs outside of the carceral system." After years of work—following a model not unlike that wielded by those of Lucha Zapoteca, and including laying out a detailed alternative vision for their community, their efforts prevailed, and the jail stopped caging people for ICE.

■■■

Budgetary resistance can also scale up. One illuminating example is Detention Watch Network's #DefundHate campaign, which, as Hernandez describes, worked as an effective national effort to curtail the growth of immigration enforcement. The coalition—made up of grassroots immigrant rights organizers, faith-based groups, and policy advocates—blocked nearly $12 billion in proposed funding for ICE and Border Patrol. The campaign's strategy was pragmatic: Rather than focus solely on moral appeals, #DefundHate targeted the federal appropriations process—the mechanism through which enforcement agencies get bankrolled by Congress. Through coordinated public pressure, coalition letters, and mobilization of political allies, activists forced lawmakers to scrutinize spending requests that previously passed without question. By choking off new allocations and blocking "reprogramming" attempts—when agencies move money internally to expand detention or border operations—the campaign transformed budget negotiations into a site of direct resistance.

The victories—in Illinois, California, and with the federal budget—were more than technical tweaks or accounting maneuvers; they represented a deliberate interruption of the machinery of detention and deportation. As migrant advocates warned at the time, unchecked ICE and Border Patrol funding fuels further abuse and deaths of immigrants. Limiting those funds means limiting reach—fewer cages built, fewer raids carried out, fewer lives destroyed. The #DefundHate campaign frames its work not just as opposition but as redirection: Every dollar denied to ICE or Border Patrol is a dollar that could support housing, healthcare, and education in immigrant communities. Defunding, then, becomes a moral and material practice of care—a way of closing camps not by waiting for reform but by cutting off their oxygen supply.

Not every community is the same, of course, and not everything is going to work everywhere. Hernandez gave the example of California's Orange and San Bernardino Counties, both right-leaning and unlikely to pass anti-detention measures. Instead, organizers focused their efforts at the state level, pushing to pass the TRUST Act in 2013, which prevents California law enforcement from holding people arrested for criminal violations solely so they can be turned over to ICE; and the TRUTH Act in 2016, which guarantees, at least on the books, further due process protections for arrested immigrants.

Part of the goal of finding ways to win, even if indirectly, Hernandez says, is so that people don't lose hope. "We are fighting for our freedom, for our right to stay with our families and communities, fighting to have life. Just knowing how many people are fighting back gives us hope, gives me collective hope. We've been through very dark periods. But we have always pushed back, forming networks and coalitions, holding each other."

My conversation with Hernandez calls to mind what Juan Ortiz said about the beginning of the fight against the Tornillo camp. "We knew it was more important to get something done than to do it perfectly. We knew we were going to be under a magnifying glass," he said, which is why it was so important to be careful and cautious.

That's even more true today. In periods of "state-created chaos, we need to be the order," Ortiz told me. More than anything, "You need an ongoing physical presence. Presence is sacred." In between his everyday commitments, including graduate school, he noted, "I'd walk out my door, directly into the struggle."

Global Camp Resistance

There's no place in the world where immigrants are locked into camps and don't fight back. Attempts to evade or escape detention, legal fights, calls home, hunger strikes, even just resentment or rancor—all are forms of resistance. So is creating life and community inside the camps. When a camp opens or expands, communities and organizations spark to life and push back. One major organization, the International Detention Coalition, has been working with UN agencies, as well as on the ground now in seventy-five countries, to try to end immigration detention. The coalition researches, puts out reports, and engages with local organizations and governments as part of that effort. One of their areas of focus has been on alternatives to detention, especially "nonrestrictive" alternatives—those that do not involve electronic shackling or other restrictive conditions. They have put research behind the obvious: Keeping people out of cages saves money, preserves free movement, and is in the community interest.

As the coalition's former director Grant Mitchell notes, research has shown that migrants with a perceived "high risk of absconding" from court dates or check-ins are less likely to do so when given basic support. "This is particularly the case," he observes, "when people can meet their basic needs through legal avenues, are not threatened with detention or refoulement, and remain hopeful regarding future prospects."[13] People will follow the law when it's not punitive or designed to marginalize or expel them.

But to understand why so many people are moving across borders in the first place—and why camps keep filling no matter how many are built—we have to look upstream. People rarely leave their homes, families, and communities because they want to. They leave because war, economic devastation, climate catastrophe, and political repression have made staying impossible.* And those conditions are not random: They are frequently produced or deepened by the same governments that then criminalize the resulting human movement. US military interventions and rapacious trade policies have destabilized economies and governments across Latin America, the Middle East, and beyond, generating the very displacement and suffering that detention systems claim to manage. As scholar and organizer Harsha Walia argues, border enforcement is not a response to a migration crisis—it is part of the same imperial system that produces one.[14]

"Our fight against detention and deportation in the US must be anti-imperialist," says Silky Shah of the importance of looking beyond just the camp system in the US. "If we continue to silo our work in the US without a clear politics against US imperialism, the conditions will exacerbate." Corporations and militaries, especially the US military—with bases in at least eighty countries throughout the world—breach borders as they please, often leaving a wake of uprooting destruction behind them. We can't effectively resist the escalating crisis of

* As of 2025, according to the UN Refugee Agency, there are about 120 million forcibly displaced people across the globe. "Figures at a Glance," UNHCR, updated November 4, 2025, https://www.unhcr.org/about-unhcr/overview/figures-glance.

forced migration—and nations' exacerbating responses to it with the border industrial complex, including a vast network of immigration camps—if we don't look beyond our own borders. The camp, at its core, is not a response to people out of place, but to a global system that displaces. To close the camp, you must take on that system.

To conclude with a lesson inspired by the Danes: "You shall protect anyone chased by ICE."

PART II

BREAKING OUT OF THE CAMP

4

ICE POWER MAP

There can be little hope of changing a system without understanding its origins, components, finances, and the people in charge. Among community organizers working in a wide range of contexts, power mapping has long been an essential preliminary organizing step to help folks understand where to direct their energy. It's basically an autopsy of a living entity—prying open the carapace to reveal the lungs and heart, then tracing the circulatory system to locate the clogs, hemorrhages, and scleroses—with the ultimate goal of healing the body politic.

Any power mapping, however, should be supplemented (see the rest of this book) with an understanding of our capacity and will to heal the ailing abuses. As Frederick Douglass put it of nineteenth-century slaveholders, "The limits of tyrants are prescribed by the endurance of those whom they oppress." In other words, what are we up for?

Now, to the map.

What Is ICE?

Immigration and Customs Enforcement is an agency under the Department of Homeland Security that arrests, detains, and deports people from the United States. That is, ICE runs the camps, whether directly or by contracting private, for-profit companies to run them at ICE's significant expense.

ICE was created in 2003 as part of the national security revamp that followed 9/11. The agency is a mash-up of the former Immigration and Naturalization Service (INS) and the US Customs Service. It was authorized as a new agency by the Homeland Security Act of 2002—the law that established the Department of Homeland Security. In outlining the primary mission of DHS, the 2002 law makes no mention of immigration or border crossings but, rather, declares that the department's stated mission is to "prevent terrorist attacks within the United States." Even under the section of the law that specifically addresses border control (Title IV–Directorate of Border and Transportation Security), the agency's first responsibility is "preventing the entry of terrorists and the instruments of terrorism into the United States." Not until subsection 3 of Title IV is immigration enforcement mentioned. The word *detention* is used in the law only five times—four of them in reference to the detention of minors, which is in the section titled "Children's Affairs" and focusing on maintaining "statistical information and other data" on detained children. Over the years, the 2002 Homeland Security Act has been amended multiple times, and, as with all laws, there are chasmic gaps between how the law is codified and how it is enforced.

ICE has various branches, including Enforcement and Removal Operations (ERO, conducting arrests and deportations); Homeland Security Investigations (HSI, investigating a host of activities, including drug trafficking, sex trafficking, money laundering, and intellectual property theft); and the Office of the Principal Legal Advisor (OPLA, made up of about two thousand attorneys and staff who mostly fight in court to get people deported or defend the actions of ICE agents). All these branches work together to police the movement of people and commodities. There have been moments, especially when ICE writ large has faced scrutiny or pushback, when HSI wanted to divorce itself from ERO. In 2025, HSI agents were tasked with prioritizing immigration arrests instead of their typical focus on smuggling and trafficking violations.

Under what authority does ICE function?

A key question concerning ICE's authority is whether such authority should exist at all. When and why did the federal government establish that it may regulate who enters the country and how, or that its agents may forcibly remove people from the country? Many trace that authority—the plenary power doctrine—to Supreme Court rulings in the Chinese Exclusion cases of the late nineteenth century (outlined in chapter 1), when justices argued that immigration regulation is not an enumerated power in the Constitution and thus is subject to limited judicial review. The justices were effectively arguing themselves out of power, and leaving it to the executive branch. Another component of the plenary power doctrine is that it is the federal government, not the states, that regulates immigration.

Immigration scholar Adam Cox calls plenary power "an invented doctrine of exceptionalism."[1] Manufactured though it may be, it nevertheless exerts extraordinary force. Attorney and immigration advocate Andrew Free notes the importance of considering where else the plenary power doctrine applies, or has applied, in US law: namely, in the realm of foreign policy, including imperial adventures abroad (as in the deadly 2026 incursion into Venezuela and the kidnapping of its president), as well as the attempted domination and extermination of Black and Indigenous people at the country's founding. Free argues we might think of immigration enforcement as something like "interior imperialism." Or, as writer and organizer Harsha Walia calls it: border imperialism.[2]

Challenges to plenary power mostly manifest as disputes between state or municipal governments and the feds. These disputes play out in fights over sanctuary policies, the refusal (or attempted refusal) of National Guard deployments within the country, or regulations of immigration detention through permitting and licensing. In recent cases where states, such as California and New Jersey, have attempted to restrict certain forms of immigration detention through legal and democratic processes, the federal government has stepped in, throwing its weight behind the plenary power doctrine to reassert their ability to cage and exile immigrants.

■■■

The specific authority for ICE officers to arrest and detain people who have allegedly committed immigration violations derives primarily from 8 U.S.C. Sections 1226 and 1357, as articulated in the 1952 Immigration and Nationality Act—a law that has been amended many, many times over the years.

Section 1226 allows ICE agents with an administrative warrant (different from a judicial warrant) to arrest and detain someone pending a decision as to whether that person can ultimately be deported. Such "ICE warrants" are issued by immigration officials. Unlike judicial warrants in criminal cases, ICE warrants don't require a judge's signature. Instead, an officer must merely establish that "there is probable cause to believe" that the person named in the warrant is subject to deportation, which often has nothing to do with criminal charges or convictions.*

Section 1226 further authorizes, pending deportation proceedings, the continued detention of the arrested person or their release, either on bond (never less than $1,500) or on "conditional parole" (the person's own recognizance, which basically means ICE trusts the person to show up to court). Bond or parole may be revoked at any time, and the person can be rearrested and redetained.

In 2025, the Board of Immigration Appeals—the presidentially appointed oversight body that hears appeals of

---

* A leaked ICE memo from May 2025 authorizes agents, in clear contravention to Fourth Amendment protections against unreasonable searches and seizures, to "forcibly enter into certain people's homes without a judicial warrant, consent, or an emergency." It's unclear how widely the memo's directive has been applied, but reporting found that new recruits were being trained on the memo. Lawyers filing suit against the directive saw it as a seismic shift from long-settled constitutional law. Rebecca Santana, "Immigration Officers Assert Sweeping Power to Enter Homes Without a Judge's Warrant, Memo Says," *AP News*, January 21, 2026, https://apnews.com/article/ice-arrests-warrants-minneapolis-trump-00d0ab0338e82341fd91b160758aeb2d.

immigration cases and guides legal practice—ruled that anyone who has entered the country without authorization is no longer eligible for bond. Noting the "magnitude of injustice" this ruling would cause, the American Immigration Council described its effect:

> The grandmother down the street who crossed the border 30 years ago? Her detention is now, for the first time, 'mandatory.' The asylum seeker who, desperate for safety, braved the desert, and later sent his information to the government in an asylum application? Mandatory detention. The countless undocumented mothers and fathers who work tirelessly to care for their children? Them too.

The council summed up their analysis: "Detention as an instrument of suffering—to coerce immigrants to abandon the legal process—is both the foreseeable result and the unstated goal."[3]

Local law enforcement agents—police officers or sheriff's deputies—can also be cross-deputized to enforce immigration violations, which are typically the jurisdiction of federal agencies. The participation of local officials in immigration enforcement is authorized by a program called 287(g), in which a local law enforcement agency signs an agreement with DHS to hand over people booked into jails, or to actively patrol for potential immigration violations. During the second Trump administration, the controversial program is expanding rapidly around the country, causing people to lose trust in their local governmental agencies. This, in turn, means that people are less likely to report crimes, and that they will sometimes go to great lengths to avoid contact with local officials.

In the first year of the second Trump administration, over a thousand additional law enforcement agencies signed 287(g) agreements with DHS, a more than 1,000 percent increase.[4] But even without such explicit coordination, ICE maintains presence in local jails. In Pima County, Arizona, where I live, which does not have a sanctuary designation but deems itself friendly to migrants, ICE routinely picks up people from its jail. In just the first six months of 2025, ICE arrested 149 people from the Pima County jail. The agency didn't need a special agreement, because everyone booked into the jail is checked against various federal databases, including ICE—a standard procedure for jails across the country.

Immigration enforcement before ICE

While immigration is not mentioned in the Constitution, the power to decide who is a citizen and who is part of the national community was initially claimed by Congress. The 1790 Naturalization Act granted any "free white person" of "good character" the chance to become a citizen. But that was about who they were letting in, not who they were trying to keep out. The latter authority didn't come until the late nineteenth century, a hundred years after the founding of the country. The 1891 Immigration Act created the Office of the Superintendent of Immigration within the Treasury Department. The superintendent oversaw a new corps of US immigrant inspectors stationed at the country's principal ports of entry. In 1895 Congress renamed the agency the Bureau of Immigration. Five years later, Congress further consolidated immigration enforcement by assigning enforcement of both Alien Contract Labor laws and Chinese Exclusion laws to the head of the agency.

Then, in 1903, Congress transferred the Bureau of Immigration from the Treasury Department to the newly created Department of Commerce and Labor. An "immigrant fund" created from collecting immigrants' head tax paid for the bureau to function. Fifty cents per immigrant financed the service at first, increased to four dollars by 1907. Two years later, in 1909, Congress replaced the fund with an annual appropriation. In 1940, INS was moved again, this time to the Department of Justice.

The jurisdictional shifts are telling: The regulation of migration was initially deemed a concern of commerce, then a concern of labor, and finally one of justice and homeland security. That is, immigration was first codified as something to regulate (and sometimes foment) under the Treasury Department, then as something to utilize (and exploit) under the Labor Department, and now as something to protect against (or to stop and punish) under the so-called Justice Department.

Who runs ICE?

As of early 2026, the acting director of ICE is Todd Lyons, who has not been confirmed by the Senate. A career law enforcement officer, Lyons has worked for ICE since 2007 and is the agency's twentieth director. Due to partisan polarization and the politicization of immigration, there have been only three Senate-confirmed directors (out of a total of twenty) in ICE's entire history—the most recent being Sarah Saldaña, who left the office in January 2017.

Tom Homan, a former acting director of ICE (appointed by Obama in 2017), is currently the Trump regime's "border czar," frequently appearing on television as a lugheaded anti-immigrant crusader.* When he appointed Homan to the position in 2024, Trump wrote, "Tom Homan will be in charge of all Deportation of Illegal Aliens back to their Country of Origin. Congratulations to Tom. I have no doubt he will do a fantastic, and long awaited for, job."[5] Homan, like Lyons, is also a career law enforcement officer, having worked as a Border Patrol agent for thirty years. In 2013, Obama appointed him as ICE's executive associate director of enforcement and removal operations. Long a proponent of family separation as a means of deterrence, he has also worked for Fox News and has consulted for, or been contracted by, camp corporations and border construction companies. In 2024, he allegedly took a $50,000 cash bribe (allegations of which he hasn't denied).

In a 2025 hiring spree, ICE offered a $50,000 signing bonus, plus student loan forgiveness, to lure in more agents. By early 2026, DHS boasted that they had more than doubled the ranks of ICE, which had jumped from around ten thousand to twenty-two thousand agents. They claimed to have received more than 220,000 applications for the job.[6]

Where and How Does ICE Detain People?

The number of operational camps in early 2026 is somewhere around 220—an increase of more than 100 camps since early 2025. ICE detains people in camps in all fifty states, as

---

* In American politics, "czar" is an amorphous term without legal definition, usually used to designate someone assigned to tackle a specific issue.

well as Puerto Rico, Guantánamo Bay, the Northern Mariana Islands, Guam, and the US Virgin Islands. The agency also consults and trains officers in dozens of foreign countries. The state with the most caged migrants is Texas, where around 18,000 people are locked up in camps, followed by Louisiana, with 8,200, and then California, Florida, Georgia, and Arizona.[7] Those numbers will very likely be different, and probably higher, by the time you read this. Nearly half of these facilities have a guaranteed minimum bed count which, as we saw in chapter 2, means the contractors are paid for detaining a given number of people even when there aren't that many people detained.

The camps come in different administrative forms, including service processing centers owned and run by ICE; contract detention facilities run by private, for-profit companies that contract with ICE; and intergovernmental service agreements, which authorize ICE to rent out space in city-, county-, or state-owned facilities.

As Detention Watch Network explains, however, "The arrangements are more complicated, and these categories can obscure the involvement of private companies even at public facilities. Service Processing Centers, those facilities owned and operated by ICE, do sometimes contract out for detention-related services such as security, transportation, and food."[8]

As of 2026, seventeen camps have a capacity of one thousand or more people, and DHS is planning eight massive new camps, each with a capacity of ten thousand.

What laws or regulations govern the camps?

According to the Supreme Court, immigration detention is formally classified as civil, not criminal. The result is that the government is legally prohibited from subjecting people in immigration camps to punitive conditions of confinement—conditions that include an "expressed intent to punish," as a 1979 Supreme Court case defined it. Yet, as Alina Das, immigration attorney and author of *No Justice in the Shadows: How America Criminalizes Immigrants*, explains in an article for the *Harvard Law Review*, the distinction is constitutional hairsplitting that offers people detained in the camps little protection from punishment.*[9] The Immigration and Nationality Act also requires federal officials to "arrange for appropriate places of detention" and to ensure, when migrants are held in local jails, "acceptable conditions of confinement." But the written detention standards that arose from this mandate—first issued by the INS in 1980 and amended six times through 2019—remain largely unenforceable and are little but nominal checks on abusive and sometimes deadly conditions. In other words, mandating "acceptable conditions of confinement" is mandating a paradox.

Federal courts have at times applied constitutional and statutory principles to release medically vulnerable detainees or order specific remedies, but more commonly, courts have rejected these cries for release or remedy outright, treating the government's self-described "mandatory" guidance

---

* Confusing the distinction between civil and criminal violations, Kristi Noem, who served as DHS secretary during Trump's second term until she was removed from her post in March 2026, said explicitly: "Break our laws, we'll punish you." Joshua Kaplan et al., "Kristi Noem-Tied Firm Secretly Got Piece of $220 Million DHS Ad Campaign," *ProPublica*, November 14, 2025, https://www.propublica.org/article/kristi-noem-dhs-ad-campaign-strategy-group.

as nonjusticiable. In several high-profile cases during the COVID-19 pandemic, as Das lays out in her article, appellate courts emphasized deference to the executive's "preeminent role in managing immigration detention facilities" and declined to find unconstitutional conditions even where, for example, COVID was running rampant and killing people.[10]

The weakness of judicial oversight stems in large part from doctrinal deference. Again under the plenary power doctrine, courts have traditionally declined to scrutinize "the wisdom, the policy or the justice"—as articulated, as we saw in chapter 1, in 1893's Supreme Court case *Fong Yue Ting*—of immigration enforcement measures. At the same time, in prison law, the judiciary gives broad deference to prison authorities on the ground that managing prisons and jails is "peculiarly the province of the Legislative and Executive Branches."[11] The confluence of immigration, administrative, and prison law has thus produced a legal regime in which courts not only extensively defer to the executive branch but also view regulation of detention conditions as voluntary and unenforceable—even when violations of these rules threaten and, in fact, grind up the most basic rights of migrants.

This structural deference has created what Das characterizes as a state of lawlessness within the immigration camp system: constitutional, statutory, and administrative protections exist in theory, but in practice they are weakly enforced or effectively hollowed out by pettifogging courts unwilling to constrain executive action.

In the days of relative decorum and nominal rule-following (before Trump's second term) there were two DHS subagencies—the Office for Civil Rights and Civil

Liberties and the Office of the Immigration Detention Ombudsman—specifically tasked with oversight duty of immigration camps. In 2019, Congress mandated the Department of Homeland Security's Office of Detention Oversight conduct inspections twice a year at camps that detain ten or more people, giving them $6.9 million for the job. While they fielded complaints and issued reports, in early 2025 the Trump administration abolished both offices. After lawsuits, the offices were restored, but staffing was reduced to their "absolutely irreducible minimum."*[12] Reporting from 2026 showed that their restoration was to little effect: Even as the number of people detained in the camps spiked, as did detention deaths, the number of inspection reports declined by 37 percent.[13]

In sum, standards are abysmally low to begin with, and the courts have taken little action to regulate or oversee the camps.

What is the role of local authorities and politicians?

Local authorities offer legitimization, licensing, and permitting for ICE camps. They allow them to exist, enabling camps through land-use and zoning approvals and contracts (especially with private prison firms). They may also provide cooperation (directly or indirectly) with law enforcement

* The total personnel for the two key oversight offices, the DHS Office for Civil Rights and Civil Liberties and the Office of the Immigration Detention Ombudsman, went from 260 staffers to merely 32. See *Immigration Detention Expansion in Trump's Second Term* (American Immigration Council, January 2026), https://www.americanimmigrationcouncil.org/wp-content/uploads/2026/01/immigration-detention-report.pdf.

and information sharing. At the same time, local officials serve as political actors who can mobilize public opinion, exert regulatory pressure, litigate, or protest, which can force changes in policy, practice, or legal status of camps.

In Louisiana in 2024, the governor ended parole (effectively early release for good conduct) for people imprisoned after August 1, 2024. But, soon after Trump retook office, Louisiana made an exception, allowing undocumented immigrants to be paroled out, straight into the hands of waiting ICE officers. Oklahoma and North Dakota began a similar practice.[14]

In the small town of Mason, Tennessee, Mayor Eddie Noeman and town's board approved reopening the West Tennessee Detention Facility under contract with ICE and CoreCivic.[15] The mayor pitched the facility as a business investment and economic development for the town. Residents balked, fighting against the camp, but the board approved anyway. While economic incentives may often drive local authorities to partner with camp operators, the case also reveals tensions: Many local residents and some alderpersons opposed the deal, raising concerns about transparency, moral responsibility, and how detention camps affect immigrant communities.[16]

The Atlanta Police Department, to give another example of local jurisdictions' role in enforcement, uses a network of thousands of license plate readers (surveillance cameras), manufactured and operated by Flock Group, to search for immigrants.[17] While local reporting didn't ascertain the results of such searches (whether or not they resulted in immigrants' apprehension), Atlanta Police's network of Flock readers was used by Border Patrol almost 3,500 times in just the first ten months of 2025.

Who Runs the Camps?

As of 2025, almost 90 percent of all people locked in immigration camps in the US are in facilities run by private, for-profit corporations.[18] Meanwhile, only 8 percent of people incarcerated in US prisons are held in facilities run by private corporations.[19] That 90 percent figure will likely be shifting, however, as immigration detention expands at breakneck speeds and the military and some states begin to build their megacamps.

ICE's Enforcement and Removal Operations (ERO) contracts directly with private prison corporations, indirectly through counties or cities via intergovernmental service agreements, or—as seen in early 2026—tries to run some camps on its own.

The biggest private camp operators are GEO Group and CoreCivic. Smaller companies include LaSalle Corrections, Ahtna Technical Services, and the Orwellian-sounding Management and Training Corporation.

There are also many companies that ICE contracts for food, medical services, transportation, surveillance, and more. Corizon Health and Spectrum Healthcare Resources provides (often the bare minimum, sometimes negligible, and occasionally no) medical services. Companies like Aramark, Trinity Services Group, and GD Correctional Services dish out the slop, typically making millions off the provision of mostly empty calories. Aramark, for example, made $1.8 million per year serving meals (costing the federal government between $1.35 and $2.25 each) at the Bergen County Jail, which houses immigrant detainees. As authors Nancy Hiemstra and Deirdre Conlon put it, "The system is based on making money off of detainees, and is set up in such a way that chronically hungry and sick detainees are part of the business model."*[20] Yet another company, Ecolab, provides cleaning services. GTL and Securus are corporations charging extortionate fees for phone calls, video visits, and commissary items inside camps.†

Who profits?

Corporations pocket billions from our nation's anti-immigration politics. ICE pays companies up to $165 a day, sometimes more, for each person held in detention. More arrests mean more money for these companies. GEO Group and CoreCivic, ICE's biggest contractor, each rake in over a billion dollars of revenue a year. In just *one quarter* of 2024, GEO Group had a revenue of more than $630 million. For just a single camp—New Jersey's

---

* Nancy Hiemstra and Deirdre Conlon, in *Immigration Detention Inc.: The Big Business of Locking up Migrants* (London: Pluto Press, 2025), offer an example of two food service bidders vying for a contract with Essex County Correctional Facility in New Jersey: GD Correctional Services and Ahtna Technical Services. "GDCS won the contract by offering meals at roughly 25 percent less than their one competitor; GDCS bid $1.43 per meal, and Ahtna bid $1.95 per meal. County records show no discussion of what a 50-cent difference in price per meal means, nor is there any mention of the many recorded detainee complaints regarding food."

† If you've ever been frustrated with bad customer service, never get locked out of your GTL account. Speaking from personal experience, their labyrinthine phone tree, monthslong delay in responding to emails, and ensuing piddle of nothingspeak ensure it is all but impossible to regain access.

Delaney Hall—GEO Group was projecting $60 million in revenue for the first full year of operation.[21] Both of these companies also lobby the government: GEO Group and CoreCivic each "donated" a quarter million dollars to the Trump inaugural committee in 2016. In 2025, CoreCivic upped that donation to half a million.[22]

GEO's subsidiary, BI Incorporated—whose tagline is "Strengthening Communities Through Innovation"—runs an ankle-shackle surveillance ("alternatives to detention") scheme, which in late 2025 was awarded a two-year contract from ICE worth $121 million.[23] BlackRock and Vanguard—asset and investment management companies running hugely popular mutual funds—are the largest shareholders for both CoreCivic and GEO Group. Together, as of November 2025, BlackRock and Vanguard own over half a billion in both CoreCivic and GEO Group stock. That is, those companies give billions of dollars to private companies to cage human beings because of where those people are from—and they are getting very rich doing so. Other companies investing in the immigration camp system include Fidelity, State Street, Goldman Sachs, and others. You can do a simple search to see if you might be part owner—and thus financial enabler—of the camps.

Local jurisdictions also cash in, at least in the short term. In Marysville, California, the town where the local jail had signed an agreement with ICE to lock up migrants before finally canceling the contract in 2022, the agreement included a minimum bed mandate of $150 per day for 150 beds. There were months when there were fewer than ten people in ICE custody in the jail—and at one point there were no people held at all—but the feds, as we saw above, continued to pay $22,500 a month, or $8.2 million per year.

Who doesn't profit?

People detained in the camps are often coerced to work for very little pay. Private companies managing ICE camps are required to offer the "voluntary work program." While participation in the program is not mandatory, ICE's own description of it notes that "essential operations and services shall be enhanced through detainee productivity" and "the negative impact of confinement shall be reduced through decreased idleness, improved morale and fewer disciplinary incidents."[24] The standard, set by Congress in 1979, is that people who are detained and working must make at least one dollar per day, which is often what companies pay.

In a 2017 lawsuit filed by people held at GEO Group's Northwest ICE Processing Center in Tacoma, Washington—previously one of the largest camps in the country, with a capacity to lock up more than 1,500 people—workers demanded at least minimum wage for their coerced labor. GEO Group complained that if they weren't able to rely on almost-free labor, they would have to hire an additional eighty-five people. The detained workers won the lawsuit, and GEO Group was ordered to give more than $17 million dollars in backpay.[25] The company appealed the ruling, and the Biden administration, in 2024, submitted a friend-of-the-court brief to the Ninth Circuit claiming that "Congress's purpose in authorizing the [Voluntary Work] Program was to foster good order in immigration detention facilities."*[26]

---

* A revealing line about the anxiety of the federal government from the Biden administration's friend-of-the-court filing: "Federal immigration detainees are in the custody of the United States. GEO and other contractors are permitted to house individuals

Johannes Favi, who was in ICE custody in Illinois's Kankakee County jail for ten months—"no sunlight, no breathing fresh air, nothing," as he described it to me—worked seven days a week. He cleaned the floors, worked the kitchen, and did basic maintenance, not only to kill the boredom but to earn enough (barely) to keep in touch with his wife, who had been four months pregnant when he was initially taken into custody. "Every Sunday I would use the seven earned dollars to call my wife, hear how her pregnancy was going," he said. Because of the extortionate fees for making calls, he only got a few minutes to talk to her.*

Local jurisdictions don't profit, either. They do get direct cuts of contracts in the short term, but as we saw in the previous chapter, numerous studies show that having a camp in town depletes the economy in the long term.

Who has access?

Sometimes—not always or consistently—family, attorneys, journalists, chaplains, and inspectors are allowed to enter

---

in immigration detention—and to permit them to work under the Program in the facility—only because the United States has granted GEO that authority."

* Favi told me he met his son by a picture sent to him by mail. After winning his release, he made a short film about his experience, became deputy director of the organization Illinois Community for Displaced Immigrants, and was integral in passing Illinois's Way Forward Act, which partially prohibits Illinois law enforcement from cooperating with immigration enforcement and offers protections for immigrants who are victims of crimes. He is also the founder and CEO of Caged Dreams, a nonprofit organization that provides innovative mental health support for immigrants.

immigration camps. Members of Congress are legally authorized to inspect camps when they deem necessary, though that authority has been contested in the second Trump administration. The same shifting group can sometimes communicate—by various restricted and often-monitored means—with people detained in the camps. Visitation access and rules vary from camp to camp, and often change. Sometimes people who work or are held in camps find ways of getting word out, usually about abuses or dangerous conditions, such as through contraband cell phones, whistleblower testimony, access to the media, hunger strike, or, at the most extreme, suicide. There are occasional jailbreaks as well. People have set up pirate radio stations to open lines of communication into camps. And sometimes, via loud rallies or blocking traffic, people on the outside make themselves heard on the inside. As Juan Castillo told me when he heard the folks from Adelante loudly rallying outside his cell in Alabama's Etowah camp: "I felt so human in the moment. I didn't feel like I was this piece of garbage that they want to get rid of from this country. It was so encouraging for me to see people like that advocating for us. And just caring, you know, just caring and letting us know that they were there for us, they were there to help us, to support us in any way they could."

Juan Ortiz told me about a similar dynamic in the camps imprisoning kids in Tornillo, Texas. A lot of the activists fighting to shut down the Tornillo camp were artists, and they decided to put puppets on stilts and perform a show so the kids could watch from over the fences. He said that as soon as they started the puppet show, the kids immediately crowded around, crying out in delight. "All the kids started running to the fence and saying, 'Gracias' and clapping and cheering. And the guards were pushing them away, trying to get them away from us, but the kids were happy. And it made me realize how deep the dehumanization is. Even I was forgetting that these were just kids. They just wanted to watch a show." They needed something, anything, that would comfort them, Ortiz explained. Organizers also kicked soccer balls over the fence. Some kids wrote their names on the balls and punted them back over.

In 2012, as powerfully portrayed in the documentary film *The Infiltrators*, two undocumented youth in Florida purposefully got themselves arrested so they could infiltrate a detention camp, organize the people inside, and fight for their release. They successfully liberated about 120 people.[27]

How Long Is ICE's Leash?

The Supreme Court has held that the Fourth Amendment's prohibition against unreasonable seizures denies ICE the use of excessive force during an immigration arrest.[28] At the same time, DHS regulations allow "nondeadly force" to be used only when an ICE agent reasonably believes that such force is needed. The regulations define deadly force as "any use of force that is likely to cause death or serious physical injury" and only permit its use when the officer reasonably believes that such force is necessary to protect the officer or others from death or serious harm. DHS regulations also prohibit the use of threats or physical abuse to compel an individual to make a statement or waive his or her legal rights.

In practice, ICE agents tackle people to the ground, draw and aim their weapons, shoot with "less than lethal" munitions, make threats, wear masks, refuse to identify themselves, and habitually run roughshod over people and their rights. They also shoot and kill them, as happened with Renee Good and Alex Pretti in January 2026 in Minneapolis.

In 2025, the Supreme Court upheld ICE and other agencies' use of racial profiling. In a 6–3 vote in *Vasquez Perdomo v. Noem*, the Supreme Court granted an emergency request from the Trump administration and temporarily halted a lower judge's order that barred "roving patrols" from snatching people off California streets and questioning them based solely on how they look, what language they speak, what work they do, or where they are.[29]*

Over a century of xenophobic policymaking, as well as decades of bipartisan infrastructural buildout, laid the groundwork for Congress in 2025 to bankroll—with unprecedented largesse—an agency led by officials who repeatedly and explicitly promised to unleash terror in American streets. That is indeed what they did, and then the courts, at least initially, gave them a wide legal shield. The ensuing onslaught was met with resistance, with communities stepping up to organize to keep one another safe, fed, protected, and empowered. Lawyers scrambled and started winning cases at the same time that journalists and residents holding up phones started racking victories in the court of public opinion. Collectively, communities put a financially bloated and heavily armed mega-agency on their back foot. That organizing didn't come from nowhere.

---

* In Justice Sonia Sotomayor's dissent, she wrote: "We should not have to live in a country where the Government can seize anyone who looks Latino, speaks Spanish, and appears to work a low wage job."

5

A PRISON TOWN SAYS NO

The federal penitentiary in Leavenworth, Kansas, looks like a medieval citadel: a squat stone facade with an iron dome and a lone American flag planted in the carefully manicured grass in front. First opened in 1906, the giant lockup established Leavenworth as the epitome of a prison town. A lot has changed in 120 years, however, and formidable fortress-like lockups are no longer how most prisons or camps present these days.

CoreCivic opened the nearby Leavenworth Detention Center in 1992. Compared to the imposing penitentiary, it looks more like a prefab distribution center; its flat tan exterior is blurred by four rows of barbed wire surrounded by unlandscaped grass and concrete. The company caged people in the prison until it closed in 2021, when the Biden administration ended most federal contracts with privately run prisons. The closure followed years of scandal—understaffing, assaults, uprisings, botched medical care, neglect, physical abuse, and suicide. Then, in 2025, with Trump back in office, CoreCivic came back to town with a pitch: In exchange for letting them reopen the facility as an immigration camp, they were offering 300-plus jobs, a million-dollar upfront "impact fee," $250,000 a year for the city's coffers, $150,000 earmarked for the police department, and over $1 million annually in property taxes. That same summer, ICE struck a rushed no-bid contract with the company for the facility's reopening, promising CoreCivic $4.2 million a month.[1] To bypass normal procurement rules, ICE declared that a "national emergency at the southern border" required immediate action and argued that they needed to reopen Leavenworth so badly because too many other jurisdictions had already refused to partner with the agency.

In many towns, especially one like Leavenworth where Trump had carried more than 60 percent of the vote just months earlier, that might have been the end of the discussion. But people in Leavenworth remembered what had happened inside that prison, and this time, they said no.

I spoke with a host of Leavenworthians pushing back against CoreCivic reopening. They described their revulsion to the company, why they decided to resist, and how critical it had proven to involve the community, focus on the local, and include a diversity of actors and tactics. Organizers repeatedly stressed power-mapping as essential for understanding where to focus. So was understanding history, in particular at a local level.

Few voices have been louder in opposition than William "Bill" Rogers, a former CoreCivic guard who worked inside the prison from 2015 until it closed in 2021. Rogers never imagined he would end up on the front lines of a campaign against detention. At fifty, when he first applied for the job, he said he "didn't even know private prisons existed." There were two qualifications, he told me, for getting hired: "You have to pass a background check, and you have to be breathing—they just need bodies." Six weeks of training couldn't prepare him for the prison floor: "You're just overwhelmed," he said of his first days on the job. "The detainees know you're new and just want to play you."

During his years at the prison, Rogers was assaulted seven times. Once, he needed fourteen stitches. Another time a prisoner stabbed him through the hand, narrowly missing his neck. Each time, he was quickly ordered back on shift. "There's no downtime, let me catch my breath, let me talk to someone—nothing," he recalled. He said in one instance he had just dealt with a violent incident and, "I literally touched the handle and another code came out: Another guy was hanging."

One death in particular forever marked him: that of Dillon Reed, a young man who died by suicide on Thanksgiving Day 2018. Reed had been left in a shower stall for over an hour—far longer than the fifteen-minute maximum, according to regulations. "The officer walked by the shower ten to twelve times while he was hanging," Rogers said. "The facility waited eighteen minutes before they called 911." He believes CoreCivic's negligence directly caused Reed's death. "That kid had me laugh a million times when I was out there," Roger's said. "He was the same age as my son. His face is just imprinted in my brain." Those memories of Reed, exemplifying a pattern of abuse and dangerous mismanagement, pushed Roger to take a stand against CoreCivic.

Marcia Levering, another former guard at Leavenworth, told me how one person locked up in the prison threw boiling water directly into her face. Another "stabbed me in the ear with a shank." She described how she and others had been left alone to monitor entire cell blocks and how the company wasn't looking out for the safety of their prisoners or staff. "They're looking out for their own self-interest, which is taking the taxpayers' money to line the pockets of their higher-ups," Levering said.[2]

Tina Shonk-Little, who was detained in Leavenworth for sixteen months, said of CoreCivic, "They don't want to do better. They are in it for profit. They could give two shits about the people. The more people they have, the better off they are because it's more money in their pocket."

I talked to Levering after she had also become an outspoken critic, advocating against the facility being refurbished to detain migrants. She was part of a quickly forming coalition of organizations rallying against the reopening by holding press conferences, roundtables, and information sessions, staging door-knocking campaigns, packing community meetings, and aligning with local, state, and national organizations. One of the groups taking up the cause was the Sisters of Charity of Leavenworth, a Catholic order with deep roots in the city. At community meetings, they passed out fliers warning about the abuses that had happened before. Ashley Hernandez, an organizer with the Sisters of Charity, lamented that CoreCivic has portrayed those who oppose the detention facility as "out-of-town" agitators. She said the coalition was full of locals. "They"—CoreCivic, with headquarters in Tennessee—"are the outside organization."

Ashley said the reason people turned against CoreCivic was simple: They were exposed to what a camp is like. "You would think it would be welcomed with open arms," but the abysmal and sometimes deadly conditions for people held there, worker safety issues, and medical abuse, Ashley reflected, were "all too much." One of the people formerly detained there, she said, was telling her that a few of the women got lice, and they weren't treated until it got so bad that *everyone* had to be treated. Even a federal judge called the place an "absolute hellhole."[3] Ashley agreed: "That's what CoreCivic is."

Groundwork educating town residents of "what CoreCivic is"—laid by ACLU and Advocates for Immigrant Rights and Reconciliation (AIRR)—Ashley said, sparked a "a mob to show up at the city commissions meeting" as they were discussing repermitting CoreCivic. The testimonies ran late into the evening, mixing policy arguments with personal histories. One man read aloud from the 1858 Leavenworth Constitution, the free-state charter that proclaimed "all men are by nature equally free and independent." Others brought photographs from inside the old facility—narrow cells, mold-streaked showers, piles of broken equipment.

That prompted a more concerted local campaign against CoreCivic: Three people, including Ashley, started meeting at a local Starbucks in the Price Chopper grocery store—just a few blocks from the Missouri River and the Kansas-Missouri border—to talk about how to creatively harness the worry about a new prison opening up. They discussed how to further educate the community, how to get even more of Leavenworth's people involved.

Not every effort paid off. When they tried to broaden the issue to a statewide perspective, hosting a panel at a library and then an immigration prayer vigil in Olathe—a large and affluent suburb of Kansas City—with the specific intent of getting "more white allies involved," the response was more subdued. At an early information panel, twenty people showed up, and only one person, a young mother who didn't want her kid living in a city that locked up migrants, said they were committed to the fight. She said the mom helped them gain another perspective: "Even though we all live in Leavenworth, we weren't sure how to reach the people where they were at."

So they hosted another roundtable to try to let the community decide next steps, held at the Sisters of Charity Mother House—symbolic as the sisters have been in Leavenworth, Kansas's first city, since the beginning and had founded the first school and health systems. They asked community members at the roundtable: What do you think is best for the city? Forty or fifty people showed up, and Ashley remembered that "people walked away feeling very empowered." They got a better idea of who CoreCivic was and started reaching out to city commissioners.

The city council, pressured by the campaign, passed a zoning ordinance requiring a special use permit for any new prison or detention facility. It was a way to force public review—and, potentially, to block CoreCivic altogether. In response, CoreCivic initially applied for the permit, but then, after seeing the rise in opposition, changed tack and argued that the prison had never formally closed, and therefore that the new permitting rule shouldn't apply. They had contracts lined up, with ICE ready to move in, and they threatened legal action.

The city filed suits in both state and federal court, claiming that "CoreCivic's mismanagement directly and indirectly impacted the City in countless ways by imposing unexpected maintenance costs on its taxpayers, unreasonably increasing the burden on the City's police and law enforcement agencies to address violent crime, and even impeding the City's investigation of sexual assaults and other violent crimes against detainees and staff."[4]

The court granted a temporary injunction: CoreCivic could not reopen until it went through the permit process.[5] But, given the political leanings of the court, residents knew there was more to be done.

Esmie T, of ACLU Kansas, who has been another key organizer against CoreCivic coming back to town, explained that "Leavenworth is a pro-Trump town. We have self-proclaimed moderates and progressives"—which is why they decided to focus on CoreCivic, not ICE. There were folks who may support jailing immigrants, she told me, but who knew CoreCivic's local track record—a conscious decision to endorse human suffering that was traumatizing for the community.

Esmie said the strategy focused less on making a general statement about immigration detention and more on city governance, about who holds "authority over their own lands." She reiterated something many organizers have told me again and again: developing a deep understanding of the local politics is key. Esmie and others also stressed the importance—often overlooked—of developing relationships with (or just learning more about) the local elected officials, as well as building trust with longtime politically active residents to gain insight into local political history.

The group fighting CoreCivic became a colorful coalition: ex-guards, Catholic nuns, immigrant-rights organizers, shop owners, and veterans. It also included a few lifelong conservatives who said that while they supported immigration enforcement, they didn't want "a CoreCivic operation in our backyard ever again."

Another group that was a part of the coalition was Decarcerate KC, an abolitionist organization based in Kansas City, a forty-minute drive away. Decarcerate KC had just come off a big push trying to stop their city from building a new jail, and their members knew that if CoreCivic opened the camp, "that will be our ICE detention facility. People picked up in Kansas City will go there," Chris Lopez, one of their organizers, told me.

That's why Decarcerate KC started "connecting the dots" for people in Kansas City. They knew they had skin in the game and wanted to support. They started having weekly meetings with the coalition pushing against CoreCivic in Leavenworth, trying to figure out how best they could plug in. Multiple people told me how much they respected and appreciated that careful approach: meeting and learning from the locals, asking how best they could be useful, coming in intentionally and in a support role. As another organizer from Decarcerate KC said, "Regular-ass people in Leavenworth are organizing because they don't want a prison anymore? Oh, sign me up."

Lopez called Decarcerate KC's work a "solidarity campaign," emphasizing the importance of understanding strategy and "meeting people where they're at." While many in the coalition may not have been abolitionist, or even anti-ICE, they were at least anti-CoreCivic, which was a stance they could get behind. "It goes back to strategy," reflected Lopez. "We might not align for our vision of an anti-ICE future, but we can talk about a fundamental distrust of CoreCivic, how they've perpetuated violence on the community."

Lopez talked to me about his abolitionist politics, and how he talks to people about it. "It's less about having a hard-and-fast nonnegotiable in that conversation, but to have that conversation at all. We can't just come in and co-opt the strategy to push an abolitionist agenda; we need to focus on shutting down the facility, which is within our abolitionist goals." He said they focused on listening and "leaving seeds of our ideas," which meant talking about the history of ICE and CoreCivic. They weren't seeking to steer the work "but to provide political education that could radicalize you."

The way they did that was by hitting the pavement and knocking on doors in Leavenworth. After multiple weekends and hundreds of doors knocked, Lopez said they identified a "genuine fear in [the] immigrant population." People were scared to put their name and address on a petition. Besides talking to people specifically about the camp, they provided other resources and handed out know-your-rights cards. They found that "people just despise CoreCivic." They also invited people to get to know their neighbors and to "reimagine what safety could look like," reminding them, "We keep us safe." As an organizer from AIRR in Kansas City told me, "You hide the medicine in community building"—dropping hints about the systemic issues with ICE and US immigration enforcement. In effect, "it's base-building." Karla Juarez, executive director of AIRR, told me that as part of their campaign against Leavenworth, they've trained three thousand people in know-your-rights workshops and have hosted talks and discussions about bilingual voter education.

Leavenworth's history lent the whole standoff an extra charge. This was a city shaped by imprisonment (including of members of the Nez Perce as prisoners of war in Fort Leavenworth in the 1870s) but also by radical politics—by abolitionists and suffragists. Susan B. Anthony lived and organized there. And during the Bleeding Kansas years before the Civil War, the proposed Leavenworth Constitution advocated for the rights of all men, regardless of race. (Women were left out.) Even in a place where prison jobs are part of the fabric of life, there was a sense that this particular chapter didn't have to be repeated.

In the end, as of writing, it looks like CoreCivic may get their way and open the camp. But the fact of the fight—the fact that this deeply conservative, prison-dependent place decided to resist—is itself a kind of victory. It reminds us that closing a camp isn't always about storming the gates. Such resistance can be quietly, stubbornly, refusing to let them open for as long as possible—and organizers often see those delays as momentary wins.

Building on those efforts—those forced delays in Leavenworth—in late 2025 and early 2026, a series of jurisdictions in Plains states blocked ICE from converting warehouses into new camps: Oklahoma City, the Choctaw Nation in Oklahoma, and Kansas City, Missouri, all passed ordinances or made enough of a stink to ban or block ICE from buying buildings.[6]

The fight in Leavenworth offers a lesson for anyone trying to close a camp—or to stop one from opening. You don't always have to start with a bunch of seasoned radical activists. You can build coalition out of shared experience and local memory. You find the veterans of the system who've seen the harm up close, the business owners who value reputation and longevity over quick cash, the clergy whose moral commitments cut across party lines. As Esmie told me, "Every day they're not allowed to open is a win."

■■■

"We can do all the right things. We can be righteous and we can do an amazing job. We can spur a Senate investigation and lay out all the harms and build support and outrage. But then somebody does this," said Ian Philabaum—holding up his hand and rubbing his thumb against his index and middle fingers—"and the economic argument trumps the legal and human rights argument."

Philabaum works with Innovation Law Lab, a legal organization that represents migrants and takes on the government-backed "industry of misery," as they describe the immigration enforcement regime on their website. Along with a crew from the Law Lab and a coalition of partners in New Mexico, Philabaum has been fighting since 2019 for the shutdown of Torrance County Detention Facility in the small rural town of Estancia, New Mexico—population just under 1,500. It's high desert, sunny and cold, surrounded by ranch and agricultural land. People like their country here—both the land itself and the nation laid over it.

The Torrance camp is a stark example of the grievous harms detention inflicts on people, the sapping dependency of a small town turned prison town, and the bizarre economics of how camps are built and managed. After dangerous levels of understaffing, a suicide, and a series of damning reports about the suffering inside the camp, by the winter of 2022 the population of the Torrance camp had dwindled to just three people in ICE custody. That was after the inspector general of the Department of Homeland Security itself had issued an unprecedented "management alert," calling for the camp no longer to be used for ICE detention. The alert called for the director of ICE to "immediately relocate all detainees from the Torrance County Detention Facility and place no detainees there unless and until the facility ensures adequate staffing and appropriate living conditions."[7]

That did not happen. Meanwhile, with only those three people locked inside, CoreCivic was getting paid their monthly minimum: just under $2 million a month to cage 505 people—502 more than were actually in there.

Over the next several years, as the detained population ticked back up into the hundreds, people detained inside washed and drank from an interior spigot meant to fill mop buckets; human waste bubbled up from floor drains; understaffing and medical neglect led to health crises, hospitalizations, and death. In the summer of 2025, Tiffany Wang, an attorney with Innovation Law Lab, told *Source New Mexico*, "Several reports indicate that stagnant human waste has sat in sites across the facility and that people are resorting to desperate measures such as fasting in order to avoid defecating and defecating on paper plates to put into the trash instead of using toilets, which they are unable to flush."[8]

The horror of those long-standing conditions, revulsion to the inflicted suffering, and the basic belief in human rights and dignity are what pushed advocates to try to shut down the Torrance camp. Yet those wanting to shutter the facility were not blind to the immediate repercussions if they succeeded.

One hypothetical outcome—even part of a potential win that Philabaum laid out for me—was getting legislation passed, New Mexico's House Bill 9, to prohibit contracts between local governments and the feds to lock up migrants. Such legislation could end up closing the Torrance camp, but it might also spur the opening of another in the state—with the feds contracting directly with one of the private prison companies instead of going through a city or county first. Ariel Prado, director of civic engagement for the Innovation Law Lab, explained that even if ICE pushed to open some other camp, that would create an opportunity for advocates to demand them to follow federal procurement rules and the National Environmental Policy Act (NEPA), which would require an environmental impact study. The result could end up keeping the total number of people detained in New Mexico about the same (albeit without slowing the rapid rise in the total number of people detained nationally), and Estancia would then suffer the loss of jobs and tax revenue without any replacement employer. A result like that would produce a moral victory—and a material victory for those who are suffering in the camp or might suffer in the future—but would neither reduce the overall number of people detained nor, necessarily, improve lives for the residents of Estancia. "We have to actually care about these people, not just the principle," Philabaum told me. "And we do, that's the thing. We really do care."

So, how to square the deep concern and respect Philabaum described for the people of Estancia with the broader goal of shutting down the camp? Their response was simple: They started listening. Together with a coalition of other organizations—including local residents—Innovation Law Lab launched the Torrance County Listening Project. Crews spent a year knocking on doors, holding forums and listening sessions, and interviewing over 130 people, all to develop the People's Platform for Torrance County. That platform includes protecting local water sources, ensuring good jobs with good pay, improving access to healthcare and emergency rooms (there is no hospital in Estancia—the closest one over an hour away), and maintaining a vibrant and welcoming community.

"I think that when entire regions develop their political economies around incarceration," Prado observed, "they cultivate systems of logic, values, subcultures, and legal contracts that support the continued use of prisons as a cruelly unimaginative 'normal' solution to public health and public safety problems, though maybe first and foremost as a source of jobs and sometimes revenue." At the same time, he noted, "there are people living nearby for whom it never becomes normal, or for whom it suddenly becomes deadly. In knocking doors in Torrance County, we've met people who have lost family members in county custody at Torrance County Detention Facility: withdrawal, untreated medical emergencies, suicide. Neighbors of the jail have their own reason to hate it. I'm afraid that when we focus exclusively on immigrants being subjected to awful treatment, we imply that other human beings deserve to be subjected to cruelty."

Folks with the listening project found not only a desire for a thriving rural community but also the toll of the dangerous lack of basic and emergency health services, as well as anxiety about the camp's potential closure.

"When we get down to brass tacks, we're challenging people's livelihoods. Nobody wants to work for a prison. Nobody trusts these corporations," Philabaum explained. Yet

CoreCivic pays "two dollars more than the local Walmart, even as they work people to the bone and are perennially understaffed."

Philabaum recognized the "impact on these communities when these places get shut down." But while there may be short-term harm when a jail shuts down, there's also what Philabaum, echoing Prado, called the "long-term harm when a town relies on a prison."

That leaves the people fighting against the camp in a conundrum. Philabaum admitted they'd been challenged by some of the locals that they aren't presenting a solution—just a complaint. As Philabaum put it: "It's hard for good things to grow in the shadow of a prison." Hard—but far from impossible. "While it's important that immigration advocacy continues and abolition advocacy continues," Philabaum continued, "it will get only as far as our ability to meaningfully engage in sociopolitical and socioeconomic change toward the benefit of everybody." Indeed, the pursuit of that shift—from resisting the threat of immediate harms to refashioning society in a more equitable shape—has been a principal challenge facing people's movements for almost two hundred years.

Historian Manisha Sinha writes in *The Slave's Cause* of the deep and multifaceted understanding that nineteenth-century abolitionists, formerly enslaved organizers among them, had of the slave system. It wasn't only about freeing the people enslaved—though that was the primary and most urgent concern—but about changing the power structure. Abolitionists were, Sinha writes, "never single-issue agitators. They linked the abolition of slavery with the plight of Native Americans, labor, and immigrants, holding no truck with nativism or racism."[9]

Leaning on that spirit, Philabaum summarized: "If we're not addressing discrimination, racism, inequality, and all these other types of social ills that are coming out of late-stage capitalism, we're going to keep running into a brick wall."

The fight can't stop at pushing back against immigration enforcement in the streets, or closing the camps, but must push toward concrete efforts to change how society is organized so camps become obsolete. The way to get there is threefold: organizing from the bottom up, bringing in more people, and leaning into moral suasion—calling out the reality that the camp system tortures people because of who they are or where they're from.

Prado and others, however, worry we don't have the power or the numbers in the immigrant rights, prison abolitionist, or environmental justice movements to force the closure of every detention camp, prison, hyperscale data center, or coal mine—all issues he sees as deeply entangled. "We need more people," Prado said. "And one way to bring in more people is to find alternatives that give people a way out—when the prison is the only job, the people who work in the prison become champions of the prison. When the prison is the only source of public revenue, the city officials relying on it become champions of the prison, even if reluctantly."

But if we articulate better alternatives, "the prison becomes redundant, and I hope more people will be able to see it for the ugly, cruel thing that it is. If one prison town can thrive after the prison closes, the hope is that it'll be easier for the next to find a path toward doing so as well."

In February 2026, as *How to Close a Camp* was going to press, the New Mexico legislature passed House Bill

9 and it was signed into law, ending local jurisdictions' contracts with ICE for immigration detention as well as terminating 287(g) programs, which deputized local law enforcement to police immigration violations. The law sets an example of how local jurisdictions can stand up to the administration. There are ways around the law, and it's not certain that Torrance or other detention centers will close—and local complications remain even if they do—but, as Rebecca Sheff, senior staff attorney at ACLU New Mexico, told me, the efforts in New Mexico "would show states and localities across the country that it is more critical than ever that we use all the tools available to us to disrupt, deter, and delay the Trump administration's immigration agenda."

Closing camps is not, at its core, an act of destruction. The only way to close them and keep them closed is to generate, with each other, something better. The first step toward doing that is often listening, which is both a rigorous practice and a commitment. We can learn it from veteran practitioners such as Ian Philabaum and Ariel Prado. And what better way to actively listen than through creative inquiry?*

■■■

Every camp begins its life with a paper trail. Somewhere in a county clerk's office, a zoning board meeting, a state

---

* See appendix 3 for a list of detailed questions to probe the local connections and vulnerabilities of each camp. The list is also online at www.haymarketbooks.org/books/2880-how-to-close-a-camp.

agency's licensing database, there's a file—signed, stamped, sometimes contested—that says, *Yes, this place can exist.* Just as every contract has an end date, there's also always a start date: a way to block from the beginning. Experience shows it's easier to stop a camp from being built than it is to shutter one already in operation. Still, every license can be revoked, every permit denied. And for organizers who want to shut down these camps, that fragile scaffolding of bureaucratic approvals can be more vulnerable than it looks.

The history of successful shutdown campaigns is rife with examples of communities prying open cracks in the walls. The following are some of the lessons gleaned from these fights:

Lesson One: Follow the Paper, Not the Press Releases

Local activists had been fighting for eight years to shut down the Berks County Residential Center in Pennsylvania, which held dozens of mothers and their children at any given time, including one 19-year-old mother who was sexually assaulted by a guard. The facility's state license to operate as a "child residential facility" was revoked in 2016, with the state citing failures to meet basic childcare standards. But the lack of a license didn't shut down Berks right away. While the county kept its contract with ICE, the revocation of its license gave the Shut Down Berks Coalition a rallying point. It proved that the state itself recognized the center as unfit for children. They finally shuttered it in 2023.

Revocation of a camp's license might not close it immediately, but it can become a political and legal weapon—an official acknowledgment of harm. And the licensing fight was just one campaign during nearly a decade of work at Berks. As two of the main organizers of the Shut Down Berks Coalition explained in an op-ed after the center was finally closed, "We united people in Pennsylvania and beyond through the fundamental belief that no matter where someone came from or how they arrived in the United States, their life is of value and they should be treated with dignity and respect."[10]

As in Leavenworth, they went door-to-door to connect with neighbors and call on county officials to stop detaining immigrants. "We drew national attention to our cause while always keeping the parents and children who were incarcerated at Berks at the center of our fight," the organizers wrote.

In 2020, they filed a lawsuit against the Pennsylvania Department of Human Services in the Pennsylvania Supreme Court on behalf of families detained at the Berks County Residential Center for failing to take emergency action to protect them from infection by COVID-19.

On March 26, 2021, Make the Road Pennsylvania and seven individual residents of Berks County sued the Berks County Commissioners for violating the Sunshine Act, a law mandating public disclosure of various medical treatment and research activities.[11] The complaint alleged that the commissioners engaged in secret deliberations relating to an ICE proposal for future use of the Berks family camp. All twenty-five immigrant families were released from Berks on February 25, 2021. It was reported shortly afterward that ICE and Berks County were planning to convert the building to a prison for adult immigrant women.

Lesson Two: Licensing as Leash

Licensing schemes—how facilities are legitimated by the state—can be an entry point for direct action.

- *License Violation*: The Karnes County Residential Center in Texas, run by GEO Group, applied for and received a childcare license in 2016 despite inspections showing abuses. Advocacy groups sued the state for issuing the license.
- *No License*: Tornillo in Texas and Homestead in Florida operated without state childcare licenses because they were on federal land, exempt from state oversight. This exemption is legal—but politically toxic once exposed.
- *Temporary License = Temporary Legitimacy*: Facilities can operate under provisional licenses, as in the Karnes County Immigration Processing Center in Texas. This gives campaigners a fixed window in which to organize for closure before "fixes" are made.

Checklist for organizers

- ☐ Identify all licenses held (state childcare, health, fire safety, business, food services)
- ☐ Research expiration dates and conditions for renewal
- ☐ Track violations and whether provisional status is in effect
- ☐ Publicize discrepancies between licensing requirements and actual conditions

Lesson Three: Permits and Utilities Are Pressure Points

Every detention center needs to physically exist—and that means building and operating permits are needed, as well as hooking up the electricity, water, and sewage.

In Florida's Southwest Ranches, it was water and fire services that stopped what would have been the then-largest camp in the country from being built. In 2011, CoreCivic (formerly CCA) wanted to build a camp with a capacity of 1,500 people. Then–US Representative Debbie Wasserman Schultz, who represented the district and would later become the chair of the Democratic National Committee (underscoring the long tradition of Democrats waffling—to put it mildly—on immigrant rights), wrote a letter urging the mayor of the neighboring town of Pembroke Pines to let residents hear CoreCivic's pitch.[12] Worried about dipping property values and facing popular opposition to the project, the city of Pembroke decided to cancel its existing contract to supply sewage, water, and fire-rescue services. That was enough of a headache to scare away CoreCivic, which canceled plans to build the Southwest Ranches camp.

Southwest Ranches sued Pembroke for damages—lost revenue.[13] After a decade-long fight, they then lost in court, and Southwest Ranches was billed with $2 million in legal fees. Today, the Alligator Alcatraz gulag is only about fifty miles due west of where the proposed Southwest Ranches camp would have been built.

Other examples include activists using city zoning laws to restrict permits for expansion in Tacoma, Washington, and the Board of Zoning Appeals in Gary, Indiana, denying GEO Group's request for a zoning variance—a permitted exception to the zoning code—to open a camp.[14] Lawsuits in New Jersey pushed into the public record the fact that the Delaney Hall camp didn't have the proper permitting. And in 2026, Maryland's Howard County, outside of Baltimore, revoked a building permit for an ICE camp. The county executive, Calvin Ball, said in response to public outpouring against the camp, "It is our responsibility as local leaders to act before harm occurs and not after."[15] At the federal level, too, legal challenges can be a formidable tool, as seen with the wielding of the National Environmental Policy Act to slow construction of Alligator Alcatraz.

Checklist for organizers

- ☐ Review local zoning maps and determine the property's designated use
- ☐ Monitor variance requests (These are public record.)
- ☐ File public records requests for safety inspection results and permit applications
- ☐ Challenge permits based on environmental, fire safety, or occupancy violations

Lesson Four: Expose Sham Inspections

ICE likes to claim its facilities "pass inspection." Recall (from chapter 2) the cozy relationship the for-profit inspection company Nakamoto enjoyed with the federal government. Inspections are often "theater of compliance": preannounced, privately contracted, and designed to avoid finding violations.

Occasionally, a real inspection cuts through the performance. For example, in 2021, the DHS inspector general conducted unannounced visits that uncovered unsafe and unsanitary conditions—exactly what ICE's own inspections routinely missed. Federal law bars ICE from funding camps that fail two inspections in a row, but the rule is almost never enforced.[16]

How to use shoddy inspections

- ☐ Push to have a member of Congress schedule a visit
- ☐ Demand release of inspection reports through Freedom of Information Act (FOIA) or state records requests
- ☐ Use failed inspections to pressure local officials into ending contracts

Lesson Five: Contracts Are Fragile

Contracts may seem ironclad, but some contain early termination clauses. Indeed, county commissioners and city councils have, under sustained pressure, voted to end intergovernmental service agreements with ICE. Even when ICE tries to contract directly with private prison companies afterward, the political cost can be high enough to deter them—driving up costs to the point of closure, as happened with the South Texas Family Residential Center in Dilley.*

---

* In 2024, ICE announced the closure of Dilley. The following year, after the Trump administration returned to office, they reopened it. By early 2026, over 750 families (a total of more than 1,300 people) were locked up in the camp. One fourteen-year-old wrote about the experience inside: "All you will feel is sadness and mostly depression." Mica Rosenberg, "'I Have Been Here Too

Lesson Six: Build the Case Publicly

Information about permitting, licensing, and contracts that allows migrants to be abused and sometimes tortured in camps is only useful insofar as it provides leverage against those stamping the approvals. You need to harness the research into a narrative, then start pressing on those levers of power. Consider your audience: Elected officials and bureaucrats may respond to points about technical violations, while the general public can rally around individual cases and lean into moral arguments, pushing officials to take a stand against the camp.

How to build a public case

- ☐ Use inspection failures or revoked licenses as rallying points
- ☐ Turn technical violations into moral arguments (If it's unsafe for children, it's unsafe for anyone.)
- ☐ Pair legal tactics with visible protest (Pressure works best when the public is watching.)
- ☐ Lean into moral arguments or faith traditions, such as the nineteenth-century abolitionist slogan "Vote like you pray"
- ☐ File public records requests; identify contracts, permits, licenses
- ☐ Attend zoning and contract meetings; collect and publicize violations

---

Long': Read Letters from the Children Detained at ICE's Dilley Facility," *ProPublica*, February 10, 2026, https://www.propublica.org/article/ice-dilley-children-letters.

- ☐ Track license and permit renewals and expirations; monitor for new issuances; respond quickly to provisional statuses or inspection failures
- ☐ Build coalitions; pressure decision-makers; prepare for hearings

■■■

Closing a detention center is rarely a single strike. It's a siege: conditions exposed through sustained communications with those locked inside, licenses challenged, permits denied, inspections weaponized, contracts terminated. Each tool alone might not do the job. But together, they make operating the camp more expensive—both politically and financially—and ultimately untenable.

In the end, the barricades of bureaucracy are always vulnerable. You just have to know where to push.

6

CREATIVE RESISTANCE

Being disturbed—even horrified—is often the first step to a shutdown. The camp depends on normalization: on the quiet acceptance that the cages, roving patrols, and deportation flights are inevitable features of the landscape. Refusing that premise matters. So does direct action: putting your body on the line, joining an organization, signing up for alerts, carrying your whistle.

You can resist the camp on-site—by blocking construction, shuttering facilities, or breaking people out of camps through legal and political campaigns. In times of legal slavery, abolitionists in Northern states overran jails where captured fugitive slaves were being held. In 1836 in Boston, a group led by free Black women stormed a courtroom and successfully rescued two women, Eliza Small and Polly Ann Bates, who had escaped slavery. And in 1851's famous "Jerry Rescue" of William Henry in Syracuse, New York, dozens of abolitionists (some armed) stormed the police station and successfully brought Henry to safety in Canada. Of the twelve people arrested for enabling his escape, only one was ever convicted.

Beyond actions at jailhouses and immigration camps, resistance also happens earlier and elsewhere: by keeping people out of camps in the first place. That work begins in the streets.

Community Defense

Street resistance starts with whoever is standing next to you. With relationships. With community, which can be built through ICE watch programs, mutual aid networks, court watches, rapid response crews, accompaniment teams, and neighborhood-based protection efforts. Such community shows up in refusal-of-entry posters taped to storefront windows, in know-your-rights cards passed hand to hand, in the reading of history for context and inspiration, and in keeping a whistle on hand.

The technology of the whistle is ideally suited to community defense. An ancient tool that depends on neither electricity nor cell signal, the whistle is simple, cheap, and easily fits in a pocket or fetchingly hangs from a neck. Unlike the clunky cell phone, its circumscribed functionality is not limited but local. Power diffuses as it extends, and a whistle is powerful because it is focused: alerting people only and specifically within its sonic reach.

Everyday resistance also takes the form of boycotts of companies that do business with ICE, and of local reporters paying close attention to what federal agents (or their local law enforcement and public officials) are doing in their cities when they think no one is watching.

People switch to secure messaging apps, use VPNs to encrypt internet activity, and build community privacy plans. They learn to track ICE—not abstractly but materially:

following flights, mapping transfers between camps, tracing deportation routes, even casing field offices and staking out staging areas. Some put up signs where ICE has made arrests, marking sites of disappearance in public space. Various groups have begun tracking ICE's license plates, and the website StopICE.net developed a license plate database. The developer of the site told the news outlet *LA Taco* that "the plate tracker helps to encourage and promote legal transparency and legal accountability, especially when they're going around, switching plates, trying to hide, trying to be undetectable."[1] In Los Angeles and elsewhere, organizers have identified hotels where ICE agents are sleeping and protested outside them—blowing vuvuzelas, ringing cowbells, and shouting into microphones late into the night. The racket has worked. In at least some cases, federal law enforcement has left to seek rest elsewhere. Vermonters have conducted similar noise demos at ICE's Law Enforcement Support Center in Williston—a 24/7 coordination center providing real-time "telephonic assistance" to ICE's law enforcement collaborators. They also flood-called the private landlord of the business complex where the center was located, making the owner realize having ICE in the office park could be a constant annoyance. Activist sleuthing led nuns in Los Angeles to cancel their contract with Enterprise after learning the company was renting cars to ICE.[2]

These efforts didn't emerge fully formed. ICE watch and rapid response crews have quickly learned that too many unverified sightings can gum up the system. Accuracy, trust, and coordination matter. Otherwise, organizers risk spreading fear instead of protection. Resistance, like repression, has a learning curve and requires careful study and planning.

Targeting ICE Infrastructure

In 2025 in Vermont, local anti-ICE organizers realized that ICE was using the commercial airport in Burlington to transport people they had abducted—moving them to states with larger camps or to deportation hubs. The organizers did what effective campaigns often begin with: research. They conducted reconnaissance, developed relationships with airport workers, traced patterns, identified leverage points, mapped who could intervene and how, and ran risk analyses. I spoke with two organizers, Leif Taranta and Julie Macuga, who were key members of that resistance. They described how coalition members started with a detailed power mapping, trying to understand "What are all the things needed to make the system work?" and then moving on to "What are all the subcomponents that make it work?" After that research, they focused on identifying where they could take action, or, as Taranta put it, "What are the things that are person-sized to stop this?" They explained that airport personnel were a key target: "Those are human beings, and we can talk to human beings at the airport," planting a seed in them that they can say no to ICE. Both Taranta and Macuga stressed the importance of breaking the work down "to something tangible, something you can touch." One approach put local officials into a particularly difficult place not to act: showing up at the Burlington Airport Commission's monthly meetings, which were typically attended by a handful of locals. When a couple hundred pro-immigrant activists descended on the meeting, explaining that allowing ICE to transport people through the airport was acting in complicity with disappearance, family separation, and torture, one of the commissioners became something of an ally.

The strategy in Vermont combined monitoring and documentation with public pressure and noncompliance. Organizers held early-morning stakeouts of ICE transport vehicles. They worked the media, generating bad press for the airport. They leaned on local officials. And they won two small but significant victories. First, the airport stopped allowing ICE special access to entrances; then, ICE stopped using the Burlington airport for transfers and deportations. When ICE shifted operations to a New Hampshire airport—raising costs and forcing the use of charter flights—the organizers shared their playbook with comrades in New Hampshire. They pushed ICE out there, too.

One result was that because ICE transfers and deportations from Vermont and New Hampshire were more difficult, detained migrants were spending more time in local jails. While far from ideal, that allowed them greater access to attorneys. In early January, Taranta told me that for the first time since they began organizing, all of the women held in one specific camp had legal representation, making it far easier and more effective to fight their deportation.

A lot of that successful work done in Vermont, Taranta and Macuga explained, came out of a history of organizing around other issues, especially anti-coal activism. Years of establishing bonds, building relationships, and honing tactics ended up building, Taranta said, "a network of people who know each other and know how to work together." With these skills already developed, they found that when ICE was juiced up and unleashed under the second Trump administration, they "just needed to apply them to a different target."

Dean Spade, author of *Mutual Aid: Building Solidarity During This Crisis (and the Next)*, echoes the thought:

"When people have been doing any kind of mutual aid work, they are more ready when the next disaster unfolds." Doing mutual aid work, that is, hones skills and builds networks. "We learn how to make decisions together, how to collaborate, how to work through disagreements, how to share things," Spade tells me. We learn who has the tools, contacts, skills, and capacities we need to stand up to an assault, make change, and keep ourselves safe. "One of the biggest problems in our society is that most people don't know how to connect to and do meaningful work in their community. People who are already doing mutual aid work are often those who bring people in and help them figure out how to stay in the work," Spade says.

Resistance can also be more confrontational. Advocates have taken out billboards, staged rallies, and put their bodies on the line to protect families and neighbors. People have tracked and blocked vans, surrounded and damaged vehicles, and formed impromptu human barricades, standing off armored cavalries. Others have doxed agents, posting their personal names and information online. (Federal prosecutors have pursued charges of conspiracy and of publicly disclosing the personal information of a federal agent in some of these cases.[3] The sentence for the latter offense is up to five years in prison.) In East Los Angeles, some groups have prepared grills and bags of chilis to burn if a large-scale raid began—planning, quite literally, to spice out ICE.

Collective Discipline

In Chicago, organizers have focused on collective discipline. Gabe Gonzalez, speaking with host Kelly Hayes on *TruthOut*'s podcast *Movement Memos*, described the work as teaching people "not only how to document and bear witness to what's happening but also [to engage in] nonviolent direct action. How do we use our bodies? How do we move collectively? How do we communicate if we're in a large group? How do we respond to their tactics as a group?" These skills, he said, were essential both for safety and for effectiveness "in a moment of great authoritarian escalation."[4]

"It's been an awful time," Gonzalez said. "But we've also seen so much grace and beauty in the people of this city."

That beauty exists alongside real harm. In Los Angeles, Chicago, Minneapolis, and elsewhere, federal authorities have fired pepper balls and flashbangs into crowds, flown in helicopters to storm buildings, driven around in armored vehicles, used explosives to blast open the front doors of family homes. Even when it's not outright murder or destruction, people have been grievously injured, blinded, and deeply traumatized as immigration agents have shock-trooped through their streets. In Tucson, I witnessed agents pepper spray and fire pepper balls at the feet of newly seated member of Congress Adelita Grijalva. A close friend in LA was shot twice with so-called "nonlethal" munitions—once at point-blank range. He shared photos: a pancake-sized black-and-purple welt on his upper thigh; a lower leg swollen to nearly twice its size from ankle to knee. He couldn't walk for days and went to the doctor to check whether his leg had been broken. It hadn't.

He described being hit repeatedly: "One time they shot so many flashbangs at me that I lost consciousness. They were exploding right next to my body. I couldn't hear. Everything was ringing. My spine was hurting."

In Chicago, Minneapolis, and Portland, immigration agents have used live ammunition. After shooting a woman, an agent in Chicago reportedly bragged: "I fired five rounds and she had seven holes. Put that in your book, boys."[5] Border Patrol's Greg Bovino, before being sidelined after widespread outrage at two citizen assassinations and unleashed federal chaos in Minneapolis, emailed words of praise to the agent following the shooting, writing, "In light of your excellent service in Chicago, you have much yet left to do!!"[6]

My friend in LA was filled with resentment and disgust at what immigration enforcement entails, but he was also struck with awe at how the community responded. "I'm so happy to be an immigrant here in Indigenous Los Angeles," he told me. "I've never felt this kind of civic pride. It's been traumatizing—my body's all fucked up in ways it's never been—but I've also never felt this invigorated. It's beautiful to see how people have responded, pretty much unanimously. I'm so proud of my city."

Why was he out there in the first place? His answer was simple: He and others were "protecting our neighbors."

Such protection also carries legal and social risk. People standing up for their communities have been kidnapped, arrested, prosecuted, doxed, and publicly smeared. In Tucson, a relatively mild protest at an ICE office that involved graffiti and minor property damage (which I attended as a reporter with my young child) prompted FBI agents to knock on doors and federal prosecutors to float terrorism charges. The charges didn't stick—but the message was clear.

In a September 2025 executive memo from Trump and a follow-up implementation memo from then–Attorney

General Pam Bondi, the administration claimed that "immigration extremism" and advocacy for open borders could be signs of "domestic terrorism." Supposed concern for extremism is darkly ironic coming from an administration that sends occupying military forces to run rampant in cities controlled by political rivals, and that tortures and kills people because they were born elsewhere.

ICE and Border Patrol don't carry out their rampages alone. They are often backed by local police departments that act as handlers, backup, or partners. Resistance thus often means confronting not just federal agencies but the entire apparatus of local cooperation that enables them.

Still, communities persist. They mark the sites of harm, holding processions or prayer meetings, stringing up flowers or playing music: standing vigil and making sure to keep vigilant. The community offers emotional support, group therapy, grieving classes, free legal advice. They wash noxious chemicals out of their neighbors' eyes and offer to take kids to school or patrol day cares to alert parents and teachers if immigration agents are prowling. They share tools for building community privacy plans, and they insist, again and again, that no app can replace relationships. Technology can assist, but it is community that protects.

Marcela Hernandez of Detention Watch Network has emphasized this point repeatedly. "The intention is to isolate folks," she says of ICE's tactics. Meanwhile, "when people feel supported, that gives community power."

Raids are designed to terrorize—to keep people from going to work, from attending school or community events, from showing up at places of worship. When people lose those connections, it becomes harder to know when and where someone was taken, harder to mobilize support, harder to fight for their release.

So organizers knock on doors. They hold know-your-rights trainings. They set up information tables at day-labor corners. They tell people: You are not alone.

This pattern repeats across the country. ICE strikes; communities respond with collective support and power. The fight is not only for release but for connection. Lucha Zapoteca in Los Angeles has become a space for leadership development—where families learn to organize bond hearings, gather letters of support, gain leadership training, and map local power.

Kelly Hayes calls this kind of work "an exercise in humility." Rey Wences, in conversation with Hayes, puts it another way: "There isn't one manual to get this done from A to Z perfectly. But we show up for our communities, for each other, and for ourselves."

The Project of Liberation

Migrant advocacy organizers in Los Angeles, Chicago, New Orleans, and Minneapolis—like nineteenth-century abolitionists before them—recognize that liberating their communities cannot be done without collaborating with resistance movements abroad to combat colonial invasion and neoliberal extraction. As Detention Watch Network executive director Silky Shah tells me, "Our fight against detention and deportation in the US must be anti-imperialist. If we continue to silo our work in the US without a clear politics against US imperialism the conditions will exacerbate." That is, we need to connect to similarly spirited movements both abroad and domestically.

Leonardo Vilchis, coauthor of *Abolish Rent* and a veteran community organizer in Los Angeles, including with the LA Tenants Union, underscores the importance of connecting—an example of just one key congruity—housing rights with immigrant rights. "Our whole idea is, how do we protect our territory?" Vilchis tells me. While, today, that obviously includes defending communities from violent immigration enforcement and the incursion of federal kidnappers, it also entails proactive organizing.

Numerous Los Angeles–based labor organizations, such as National Day Labor Organizing Network, Pilipino Workers Center, and the Los Angeles Black Worker Center, have built on the city's long history of resistance with rapid mobilizations and responses since the onset of the 2025 immigration crackdown. They and other groups have joined forces with the faith community, new media (including *LA Taco*, *Boyle Heights Beat*, *LAist*, and others) as well as local politicians—what activist Bill Gallegos called in *The Nation* "fierce and effective local opposition"—to keep watch, conduct trainings, stand up to ICE and Border Patrol, and protect their neighbors.[7]

While many of those organizations have been community-building for years, or even decades, not every city or state has that history. In those cases, the best place to begin, Vilchis argues, is to forge relationships at the building level, going door to door, then at the neighborhood level, up to the community level, and finally to city and state.

Vilchis explains that organizers in East Los Angeles leaned on work done during the COVID-19 pandemic when they started food distribution networks, helping to keep people in their jobs and avoid evictions, even conducting rent strikes.

"There is a lot of talk about defending and fighting back," Vilchis tells me, "but nothing about solving the needs of the people who are displaced or who run the risk of being deported. That has to do with economics, canceling rent, getting food and other supports for families who don't have jobs."

"We go through a kind of natural process," he explains. "First you try to make sure that people stay in their home, and they know their rights and can improve their housing conditions when they're dealing with slum conditions so they can defend themselves against evictions. Then, as we address those problems, you start looking outside on the street to issues of safety." Broken streetlights, shattered sidewalks, dangerous intersections—they make up what Vilchis calls "the practical stuff about the everyday life of the community." He says that at the same time, they're generating a place where "the priorities of the people who live, work, and play in the neighborhood are the ones who are implementing them."

The pattern isn't just "ICE strikes; communities respond," but that when ICE strikes, communities that for years have been cultivating networks and power—building by building, block by block—are the most prepared to take on ICE. These groups both recognize, and *feel*, how the fights against landlords, gentrification, abusive bosses—or profligate resource extraction—and immigration agents are all connected.

In Chicago, the president of the Chicago Teachers Union, Stacy Davis Gates, has invoked the city's long tradition of resistance—from nineteenth-century refusals to cooperate with fugitive slave patrols to Pullman porters carrying news of freedom southward. "175 years ago the people who occupied the seats in city hall voted in a resolution to refuse to cooperate with fugitive slave patrols. They created liberty associations to keep each other safe and free." She describes how, decades later, Black Pullman porters shuttled newspapers back and forth to Mississippi "to tell of a place that was free of the tyranny and fascism of Jim Crow. And they turned Chicago into a Black metropolis."[8]

"Chicago has been neck-deep in the project of liberation for a long time," Gates adds.

Historical horrors are too often recognized as such—except by the people who suffer them directly—in hindsight. Today, we acknowledge the obvious moral catastrophe of chattel slavery, the racial fascism of Jim Crow, and past instances of genocide, but many people living at the time of those atrocities let the conduct persist, be legitimized in tepid debates, or hide behind the aegis of legal order. The current reality in the United States shouldn't need to descend into such widespread hate and harm before we recognize the urgency of the moment: We must not mince words, hesitate, or let ourselves or our neighbors fall prey to the creeping spread of the camp.

And yet, resistance that endures is rooted not just in opposition but in deep care—in the everyday work of keeping each other safe, connected, and unafraid to stand together in public.

CONCLUSION

RISKING OUR NECKS

In 2013 I was living in LA, organizing with DREAM Team Los Angeles (DTLA), a youth-directed immigrant rights organization headquartered in the UCLA Labor Center in MacArthur Park. We engaged in direct actions, mutual aid, political pressure campaigns, and sometimes civil disobedience. As the Obama administration was doubling down on immigration and border enforcement and continuing its surge of deportations, community members, including some family members of DTLA youth organizers, were getting snarled in the nativist nets. In coalition with a number of other organizations, DTLA decided to escalate its tactics, targeting an abusive camp on the outskirts of LA: the Adelanto ICE Processing Center.*

* In a damning DHS inspection from a few years later, the facility was found to be dangerously filthy, unresponsive to basic medical needs, and heavily reliant on the use of solitary confinement. US Department of Homeland Security, Office of Inspector General, *Management Alert—DHS Lacked Sufficient Controls to Ensure Timely and Accurate Reporting of Sexual Assault and Sexual Harassment Complaints at Immigration Detention Facilities*

For well over a month, we hatched plans about how to block a gate out of which deportation buses motored, thus stopping—for at least a day—the deportation of anyone from the Adelanto camp. The way we decided to do that was to chain people to the mechanical gate. The particulars of the tactic still haunt me: The volunteers would be chained to the gate with bicycle U-locks around their necks. My specific role was to secure a lock around both a bar of the gate and the neck of a young "DACAmented" woman named Dianey. While we all risked possible arrest, Dianey—who would be chained to the gate along with two other young women—was particularly vulnerable. Because she had only temporary legal status under Deferred Action for Childhood Arrivals (DACA), protection which can be removed if someone is convicted of a crime, she faced the prospect not

---

(OIG-18-86), September 18, 2018, https://www.oig.dhs.gov/sites/default/files/assets/2018-10/OIG-18-86-Sep18.pdf. One shocking finding by inspectors was that there were multiple nooses tied up and hanging from vents in some of the cells. According to the inspectors, "The contract guard escorting us during our visit removed the first noose found in a detainee cell, but stopped after realizing many cells we visited had nooses hanging from the vents." A Detention Watch Network report described "maggots in ground turkey meat, hardly any access for inmates to the outdoors, and, most disturbing: "straitjackets and solitary confinement were used to punish and deter immigrants from reporting mental health issues." Detention Watch Network, *Expose and Close: One Year Later; A Report on Immigration Detention in the United States*, https://www.detentionwatchnetwork.org/sites/default/files/reports/DWN%20Expose%20and%20Close%20One%20Year%20Later%20Report.pdf.

only of arrest but of being locked up in an immigration camp herself. She was also risking severe harm or even death: The gate could accidentally—or purposely—be opened while she was still neck-locked to it. (I feel, and have always felt, incredibly conflicted about the decision to lock those people by the neck.)

Dianey and I barely knew each other, but in the weeks leading up to the action, we practiced dozens of times. We would run to a different but similar fence in LA, me holding the opened U-lock with the key already inside its hole, her shuffling down to the fence and leaning her back against it, and me quickly—trying to be gentle—locking her by the neck. On my own, for nights beforehand, I practiced quickly unlocking it again and again, just in case . . . I didn't want to think in case of what.

After growing up in the Mexican border town of Juárez and migrating with her parents to the US when she was eight, Dianey was granted temporary legal status after qualifying for an initial two-year reprieve when President Obama issued the June 2012 executive order that created the DACA program. But despite her newfound ability to obtain a driver's license and access a host of other basic necessities usually reserved for citizens, she still felt a palpable fear in the community. "We're not safe," she told me. "Both of my parents are undocumented. It's always in my head." Sometimes Dianey had to drive her father, who didn't have a license, to his job. At the time, he worked in an area where the family "constantly hears stories of raids."

On the day of the action, the initial lockup went smoothly. After securing Dianey to the gate, I joined a crew of protesters and surrounded the three women, giving them shade and support, chanting and holding signs as we stood in solidarity with those trapped inside, blocking the deportation buses.

The three women—wearing matching denim jackets, black jeans, the same white T-shirts, and the U-locks around their necks—referred to those inside as their "mothers, fathers, brothers, sisters, and cousins."

Pretty quickly, two dozen sheriff officers, stern-lipped and wide-eyed through their riot-helmet visors, holding batons in front of their chests, pushed the protesters away from the gate, leaving the three chained women by themselves. Behind the sheriffs, two officers were dressed in military-green bomb-squad outfits, one of them holding what looked like a tear-gas grenade launcher. At first the three women, holding hands, continued to chant, "Undocumented and Unafraid!" but soon, under the empty desert sky, with the rest of the protesters pushed out of view, they quieted. Dianey later described more than ten GEO employees coming and ogling them from inside the fence. There the three remained, locked by the neck, until firemen eventually cut them first out of the gate, then ripsawed through the U-locks still around their necks. Nobody was deported from Adelanto that day.

At one point during the protest, with a hundred or more activists chanting "Undocumented and Unafraid!" "The Power of the People!" "¡Sí se Puede!," a few of the detained men inside the facility, hearing the raucous chanters outside, started banging on their opaque, embrasure-like windows. The brief connection between protesters and people detained inside sparked a burst of energy.

A source who worked in the camp, who wished to remain anonymous for fear of retaliation, told me that during and after the protest, the facilities were locked down. All phone calls were canceled, detainees were confined to their rooms and not let out until the evening, court proceedings for the day were canceled, and lunch was served in paper bags inside the dorms instead of in the cafeteria.

Dianey and the two other women were booked and first spent thirteen hours in a prison in nearby Victorville, then were sent to another prison. One of the other protesters was told by a GEO official that they would make sure that the women got criminal records. Dianey initially faced misdemeanor failure to disperse, trespassing, and a felony charge of vandalism. The vandalism charge was later dropped. When she was finally released the morning after the protest, she said, "I just ran out and cried like a little girl. [The detention camp] is an ugly place."

A Layer Cake of Bureaucrats and Politicians

How did it come to this? Why did Dianey literally risk her neck that day? What was she pushing back against, and why take resistance to such an extreme?

The answer is both ideological and practical. Along with a deep base of xenophobia and racism—as well as fear-fomenting politicians—a camp needs an actual building and a plot of land, which means its operations can be physically blocked or stalled. That building and land use also requires permits, sales, and the cooperation of a wide range of actors: A camp doesn't just exist—it's constructed and maintained by hundreds of signatures, inspections, and backroom approvals. And each bureaucratic strata is a point of both responsibility and vulnerability. Besides the politicians pushing for the camp and the camp operators, there abound a host of secondary and tertiary players (and targets): contractors, insurers, permitters, inspectors—the whole vertical range of the political class that can either rubber-stamp or prefer not to.

The Adelanto ICE Processing Center thus stands not just on Mojave Desert ground but on this tall layer cake of business and bureaucratic transaction. Each approval, each signature, each vote in favor is a point of complicity. Understanding this map of responsibility is critical. To close a camp, one must understand how it, and indeed the whole system of camps, was built. (See appendix 1 for a detailed examination of how Adelanto was built.) Every kind of resistance to the camps—at the sites themselves, as well as on the streets and in the halls of power—offers lessons for how they can be undone.

A CAMP IS A MAN ON HUNGER STRIKE WITH A HUNDRED OTHERS WHO LOSES TWENTY POUNDS IN ONE WEEK AND WRITES IN A LETTER: "WE WILL GET FREE OR DIE TRYING."[1]

A CAMP IS DOZENS OF PEOPLE SPELLING "SOS" WITH THEIR BODIES FOR THE NEWS HELICOPTERS OVERHEAD.[2]

A CAMP IS A MAN WRITING A NOTE ON A SLIP OF PAPER, WRAPPING IT AROUND A BOTTLE OF LOTION, AND HURLING IT OVER A CAMP FENCE TO COMMUNICATE WITH THE OUTSIDE. "IT'S COLD HERE ALL THE TIME AND THE FOOD IS POOR," THE NOTE READS. "FOR 280 DAYS WE HAVEN'T EATEN A SINGLE PIECE OF

FRUIT, BANANA, APPLE, ORANGE, OR ANYTHING FRESH. WE ARE ALL IN ONE BIG ROOM WITH NO DOORS OR WINDOWS. WE CAN'T SEE ANY GRASS OR TREES. WE ARE ALL CONSTANTLY SICK."[3]

Mudding Up the System in Arizona

In late October 2025, Evy McDonald heard news that an ICE detention camp might soon be locking people up near her home in Marana, Arizona—a small suburban ranching town north of Tucson. Given Arizona's history of targeting immigrants, as well as the Trump administration's Gadarene rush to arrest and deport as many people as possible, Evy was concerned. The facility in question was an old state prison, having sat idle and empty for years at that point, though it would be relatively quick and easy to refurbish it to start jailing migrants. Evy, seventy-four, decided to go to a community forum organized by a county supervisor for locals to learn and ask questions about what might be coming. "I thought maybe there would be a handful of people to show up," Evy tells me. But when she walked into the building—the overpacked lunchroom of the Coyote Trails Elementary School—she felt like she had "walked into a sea of hope."

What was planned as a small community event was bursting with over 350 people filling every seat, lining the walls, and spilling out the doors. Outside, folks were parking in a gravel lot down the street for lack of spaces. Four presenters from local and national community and migrant organizations sat on the stage and laid out the basics of what was happening: The state of Arizona had sold the former prison to a private, Utah-based prison profiteer, Management and

Training Corporation (MTC), which runs fourteen prisons across the country, as well as one in Australia.[4]

Despite the crowd being overwhelmingly against an ICE camp moving in—attendees jeered, hooted, whistled, and booed at the prospect—the experts walked through how, because it was a private sale, the permitting and licensing were mostly already in place and there were few legal maneuverings to stop MTC from opening their doors to ICE.

That didn't satisfy. In fact, it seemed to energize the crowd. Speaker after speaker—a former prison guard, a high schooler, a retiree, a rancher—lined up to ask questions and throw out ideas: How could this have happened? Why did the state sell to a private prison company? What can the town council do? Can *we* occupy the building? Can the owners of neighboring properties do anything to make ICE's work harder or less efficient?

Both community members and the presenters answered: Call your elected officials, call MTC, make clear to everyone involved that an ICE camp in town is intolerable. "Just keep bothering people," one of the presenters said. The evening ended with a promise of more such forums, that the community would stay on top of the issue and explore ways to push back.

Evy, who has been an activist and protester for half a century, hopes younger folks will learn from the lessons of prior generations. As she has learned from the struggles she's participated in, even after a setback, the fight never stops. "If the detention center opens, we can still disrupt things," Evy insists. "You have to be willing to put your privilege and your life on the line."

Such a spur to action, however, may seem abstract: Put your life or privilege on the line how? Where and when, with who else, and for exactly what? Or, as Evy asks, searching for creative ways to put a halt to the harm, "Is there a way to mud up the system?"

This book has sought to show how communities have done precisely that. It may not always lead to immediate shutdowns or permanent victories, but creative, community-based resistance to the camp helps us, simultaneously, begin both to dismantle them and replace them with something better. Abolition is a practice, something kindled, maintained, and ultimately won by the relationships we form and the communities we forge. Minneapolis in late 2025 and early 2026 stands as a prime example, modeling a community-focused way for people in the city to care for each other even as they're fighting the camp and its tentacles in the streets.

Lessons from Minneapolis

Meeting the ostentatious brutality exhibited by the federal government, the community response in Minneapolis has been fast and fierce. Within days of the onset of the December 2025 federal surge, immigration agents could barely take a step in some neighborhoods without being swarmed by people protecting their communities. In subzero temperatures, those community members have kept watch, countersurveilled ICE, developed almost-immediate rapid response networks (divided into nearly block-by-block areas for efficiency), set up quasi-checkpoints (or filter blockades) to identify ICE vehicles, monitored schools, built safe houses, engaged in mutual aid and widespread food and medicine distribution, and conducted a massive general strike in which as many as three hundred thousand people refused to work or otherwise withdrew from the economy.[5] Participation in these and more efforts in Minneapolis has been, in some neighborhoods, nearly unanimous, inclusive of a vast array of people and abilities. Sometimes the response was granularly organized; at other times it was almost ferociously spontaneous. The community has been agile—quickly adapting to ICE's different approaches and tactics—and has inspired other cities facing similar invasions. And while the most visible of these responses may be the outpouring of ICE watch networks in the streets, the less seen mutual aid programs may be even more extensive. Food and pharmacy distribution, medical and mental health care, education, childcare and eldercare systems, and religious services have all developed as grassroot shadow industries to keep each other safe, fed, stable, and, given the circumstances, as healthy as can be expected—a widespread system of care.

That profuse outpouring of spirit and the many-branched mobilization have been so nimble and effective when it counted because they have been built over decades, arising from a long lineage of community networking and protection systems.

The community groups in Minneapolis seen defying immigration raids in 2026 are largely a reactivation of neighborhood groups that banded together during the George Floyd uprising in 2020, when people took to the streets and changed the way millions understand racism and policing. In those months, participants went far beyond protest and demonstration: They served as community protectors and even emergency response crews, turning out when municipal services wouldn't. And that posture of community responsibility in 2020 also had precedent: not only in decades of labor and immigrant rights organizing but in Indigenous activism and resistance. In 1968, in South Minneapolis, the American Indian Movement was born in reaction to that era's racism and police brutality. AIM, which then flowered across the country and included major occupations of historical Lakota lands (Mount Rushmore, the Pine Ridge Indian Reservation, Alcatraz, and elsewhere), also established street patrols in Minneapolis. Some of the children of those original AIM patrollers are now engaged in ICE watch on the same streets.[6]

Leaning into decades of organizing to effectively resist a current assault certainly helps, but that history had to start sometime. And that sometime can be now. In Marana, some of the people who rallied with Evy against the new ICE camp there had been warmed and limbered up—forging community ties and building organizing networks—as they pushed back against a proposed hyper-scale data center that an out-of-town developer was trying to build close to Tucson.

The Vermont organizers who successfully pushed ICE out of the Burlington airport told me their particular strength had come from a history of queer mutual aid work, including providing community defense at queer events. They had fostered a crew of people who knew and trusted each other. Those relationships and that trust were what enabled them to push ICE out of the airport: They are how we slow the camp down, and how we ultimately shut it down.

One of the other takeaways from Minneapolis—and from Vermont, Marana, Chicago, Los Angeles, Florida, and elsewhere—is that our efforts are worthy, important, and even inspiring, but they are not enough. On their own they will not change the underlying conditions that enable the camps. To take one illustrative example: In February 2026, border czar Tom Homan announced that the anti-immigrant operation in Minneapolis would be scaling down and ending—a decision celebrated by many as a victory for on-the-ground organizers. But the inconvenient reality is that these ends were achieved only at the expense of a Faustian bargain: In exchange for leaving Minneapolis, the feds had arm-twisted—via threats and murderous terror tactics—local municipalities throughout Minnesota to deepen future cooperation to hand over immigrants.

The problem may be, in part, that organizers must pick a broader target—not in lieu of an immediate project of resistance or activism, but in addition to it. We can't just organize groups of people to resist a camp or respond in the moment to an ICE raid. Individual or even collectively specific acts of compassion or resistance, while critical, are simply not enough to close a camp and keep it closed, let alone close them all.

The Long Haul

Historically, political organizing in the United States has been too inconsistent, too single-issue, and simply not powerful enough to break through toward systemic and lasting change—not just to combat a single ICE incursion or operation but to abolish the agency and what it stands for: the selective policing of human mobility.

Getting that done will likely take years, if not decades, of sustained pressure and community building. From the original abolition movement and the suffragists to civil rights, Native rights, the Black Panthers, Occupy, the George Floyd uprising, #MeToo, and others—those movements' successes and failures should be lessons.

"My experience in the United States is that resistance goes in cycles," says Leonardo Vilchis, veteran immigrant rights activist and tenant union organizer. He explains to me that part of the problem has been that US political movements are built to achieve certain goals, and once one or some of these goals are achieved, it's over. Then the leadership, the movement, and the institutions move on, and "a more transformative vision is lost."

What's too often missing, he says, is long-term vision. He offers an example of the fight led by Central American refugees in the 1980s for Temporary Protective Status. He said that after they achieved their specific goal, their fight evolved to defend TPS, and that was it: "No more about transforming the rights of the immigrants."

"It's also the intergenerational thing," Vilchis reflects. Too often, a new generation begins a movement, burns out or moves on—or doesn't find younger people to guide and mentor—then, the next generation starts close to scratch and has to begin the cycle again. There are plenty of instances where that's not the case, and too often there are generational chasms instead of bridges. "This seems like it has to always be something started by new young people. There are very few people my age still doing this kind of work," Vilchis said.

Another problem is the occluding focus on elections. The tension between the sputtering trajectory of electoral politicking and the needle-moving power of grassroots organizing isn't new. The country's first abolition movement was a popular movement long before it became an executive proclamation. Enslaved people escaping to freedom and radical abolitionists pushed the country to confront the crisis of slavery long before members of Congress or Abraham Lincoln ever did.* Today, the #resistance Democrats who declare themselves to be on the side of reform have not achieved justice for migrant communities. In fact, their selective and politically opportune outrage—and their both-sidesing of human rights—have set the stage for today's Trumpian excess.

Kenia Alcocer, an undocumented organizer with the Union de Vecinos—and a frequent collaborator with Vilchis—underscores the critical importance of pushing beyond short- or medium-term goals. Alcocer was deeply involved with the fight for DREAMers (undocumented youth) during the Obama administration. But she saw the limitations of obtaining provisional status, which is what Deferred Action for Childhood Arrivals provided. She tells me that she and fellow undocumented youth began to realize that even if they obtained legal status, that limited protection wasn't going to solve many of their underlying problems. She observes, "If we don't have any economic wealth, our lives are always going to be shitty." Which begs the question: "Is citizenship enough?" Her answer is a resounding *no*. Without access to material wealth, control of the means of production, and full rights in an equitable and healthy society, even gaining citizenship status can only be a partial remedy.

Anarchist anthropologist David Graeber wrote a 2008 essay, "The Shock of Victory," that helps us see beyond piecemeal or electoral victories.[7] In it, Graeber analyzed a couple

---

* As late as 1861, Lincoln worried that the abolitionists would "upset our applecart."

of different organizing campaigns, including the global justice movement, which staged major actions in 1999 against the World Trade Organization in Seattle and against the International Monetary Fund and the World Bank in Washington, DC, and elsewhere. Despite the movement behind those protests having fizzled, Graeber argued, it was not because they were quashed but because they won so quickly—at least their medium-term goals. Briefly consider a few of their targets: the free trade agreements wreaking havoc on laborers from Chiapas to Detroit and beyond; the World Trade Organization; and the International Monetary Fund. While some major free trade agreements have been signed since, the United States hasn't since signed one of the multinational blockbuster deals that marked the 1990s. The WTO came out of the protest movement even more bruised, and the IMF, increasingly irrelevant, has been guttering for decades. Those victories are often written out of history. And while they are clear wins, the ultimate objective—rewriting monetary policies to end extractive and predatory practices that favor the wealthiest countries and corporations—obviously hasn't been achieved, as inequality and financial rapacity have only accelerated in recent years.

"The next time we plan a major action campaign," Graeber wrote, "I think we would do well to at least take into account the possibility that we might obtain our mid-range strategic goals very quickly, and that when that happens, many of our allies will fall away."[8] A mid-range win today might be pushing Trump out of office, replacing his administration with a more moderate one that doesn't deploy masked thugs to kidnap our neighbors. That "win," however, leaves a lurking danger—the loss of momentum as some allies lose focus, a profligately funded federal agency that is still designed to hunt down and arrest people, and the vast infrastructure of camps.

Which is why Vilchis, Alcocer, and others emphasize building power from the neighborhood level up, forming coalitions with those being targeted—with the people, as Graeber put it, "who don't need to be convinced that the system is rotten, only that there's something they can do about it."[9] That's how anti-ICE and anti-camp movements can turn into a positive movement to achieve systemic change: convince people there's a better, more just, open, and equitable world we can build—and keep pushing. That's how the movement will avoid running out of steam if there's a ballot-box "victory" in 2028 or 2032.

Electoral politicking—hoping on a hierarchy—is outsourcing our own safety and abdicating our self-organizing. Our elected officials built the systems of incarceration and inequality in the first place. Not all of them, of course. But the electeds are the ones who wrote the laws, approved the funding, and built the camps. Making change through them will come about not because they necessarily believe in the change but because we give them no other option. At least for now, our political horizons may be constrained by representative democracy within nation states, but that should not mean abrogating responsibility for care, or neglecting to build the structures and form the networks that communities need to keep ourselves safe and thrive.

"Right now, it's hard. Right now, it's scary. Right now, we don't know what the hell is going on," Vilchis acknowledges. "But everybody who's going through this process is going to fight back." The organizations responding now will have the capacity—and hopefully also the will and the longevity—not only to push ICE out of their communities and close down the camps but also to build something better in their place.

Is that hopeful thinking? Yes, and it's also what we need. Scaling back excesses isn't enough, because so much of the infrastructure has already been built, and more is being constructed for future and possibly more draconian excesses to come. We need to look beyond this administration, Silky Shah told me, even as we respond to the emergency that it is.

As we work to counter current and past assaults, it is essential that we use them as opportunities to learn and organize. The best way to do that, or to at least start doing that, is to read up and to show up: to talk to, to get to know, to rely on and be reliable for your neighbor.

Rümeysa Öztürk

On March 25, 2025, six plainclothes ICE agents abducted 30-year-old Tufts student Rümeysa Öztürk off the street in Somerville, Massachusetts. It was approaching dusk, and Öztürk had left her home to meet friends for the iftar meal, breaking her daylong Ramadan fast. She was holding her phone in her hand as she was talking to her mother in Turkey. A backpack on her back, she wore a mauve hijab and a long white coat. A man dressed in all black with a black hat approached and blocked her way. Five other agents, some of them in masks, all quickly surrounded her. The man in black snatched her phone out of her hand, twisted Öztürk around, and started to pull off her backpack. One of the agents said, "We're police." As she called out in protest, they pulled her hands behind her back and cuffed her.

Öztürk said she thought the people were vigilantes and that she was being kidnapped. On the other end of the line, her mother heard her scream. "As my body shook with fear, I found myself drowning in thoughts," she later wrote in an essay about the incident. "I began my final prayers."[10]

Öztürk had been conducting research for her doctoral dissertation in the Department of Child Study and Human Development, on how adolescents and young adults use social media in positive and prosocial ways. Along with three other students, she had written an op-ed in March of the previous year for her university paper, *Tufts Daily*, calling on the university president to abide by three resolutions passed by the Tufts Community Union Senate, including acknowledging the genocide against Palestinians. For that act she was doxed by a right-wing online group, threatened multiple times with death, and then finally arrested and tortured in an immigration camp. Secretary of State Marco Rubio referred to her as a "lunatic."[11]

After Öztürk's initial arrest, officers shackled her by her hands, feet, and waist, transferred her to different sites—from Massachusetts to New Hampshire to Vermont—for interrogations conducted by unidentified men, some in uniform and some not. One group so unsettled her, Öztürk wrote, that she "was sure they were going to kill me."[12] She was held incommunicado for nearly twenty-four hours, during which she suffered an asthma attack.[13] The following day, agents loaded her onto a plane and then flew her to Alexandria, Louisiana, where she was locked into the South Louisiana ICE Processing Center.

In the Louisiana camp, a nurse told her, "You need to take that thing off your head," and then removed her hijab without asking. She began wheezing—one of multiple asthmatic episodes to come. She asked for help but was unattended.

Inside the camp she was met with bad food, frequent threats, mocking guards, no sunlight, no medical care, no sleep, and no freedom. "Despite these awful circumstances," she later wrote, "I clung to my belief in humanity."[14]

Creating Community Inside the Camps

What remained for Öztürk and the other women she was detained with, what kept them going, was each other. They formed community. She recounts that when she first entered the small cell where she would be confined for the next six weeks with twenty-three other women, they greeted her "with warmth and smiles," explained to her where the few clothes they were afforded were kept, how to deal with the guards, how to do laundry, and offered her a few of the meager snacks they'd hoarded. Though they didn't have consistent access to hygiene products or even toilet paper, the women made do, supporting each other.

The legal director of ACLU Louisiana, Nora Ahmed, who has visited people in the same camp where Öztürk was held, describes the solidarity that often thrives inside the cages: "Such stories of support are legion."

Ahmed, who estimates she's met with a thousand people who have been through immigration camps, tells me that, along with the profound suffering, she sees inside a "resilience in the human spirit." Those locked inside the camps find ways to, as Ahmed puts it, "uplift people in their darkest moments."

"Over the next six and a half weeks," Öztürk wrote, "I found myself immersed daily in the love, beauty, resilience and compassion of these women. . . . We each found ourselves trapped in our own individual nightmares, but we found comfort and relief in one another."[15]

After weeks of petitioning, she was finally able to secure a small diversion to help pass the time: a cookbook. In its pages she found handwritten notes of hope and strength from the women who had read it before her. She read recipes for food she couldn't cook, dreamt of delicious meals as she was dished innutritious slop. And yet she was still spiritually fed: "It's incredible how human beings can find ways to uplift each other, transcending time, space and borders if they want to and if they choose to," she wrote.

Of the immigration camp experience, she asked, "How can suffering and compassion coexist in the same environment?"

Moments of suffering are precisely where such compassion begins. Indeed, suffering is what prompted each of the stories of resistance in this book. Compassion in Leavenworth, Los Angeles, Eloy, Marana, Dilley, Etowah, Irwin, and elsewhere—as lived and practiced by Fred Tsao, Juan Ortiz, Silky Shah, Leonardo Vilchis, Nora Ahmed, and Johannes Favi; that of the people of Minneapolis and Chicago and elsewhere doing the work—sometimes dangerous, and often mundane and invisible—of protecting their neighbors; the compassion that becomes solidarity and builds community bonds, strength, and, eventually, shared power.

Lasting resistance can start with a moment of such basic sweetness as leaving a note of hope in a cookbook. It can spark by wearing a whistle and stepping outside to protect your neighbor. But it must go beyond. The vast and rapidly growing infrastructure of the camp exists to enforce divisive hierarchies and exclusion. As long as there are camps, they will be used to cut ties between us. Compassion—along with its collective transformation into solidarity and action—is how we remake and strengthen those ties. When we are bound together as a community, there is not enough space between us for the camp to exist.

■■■

The threat of the camp is not idle, abstract, or in the future. It is now. While the threat is concentrated on otherized populations, anybody and everybody is a target. You are a target.

While camps used to take years to erect, they're now building them in mere weeks, trucking in tents, trailers, and generators, converting military bases and abandoned warehouses to detain our neighbors, spending billions on bloating the camp system. Despite the increasing ease of throwing up prefab concentration camps, their physical infrastructure is expensive, extensive, and dependent on a network of financiers and bureaucratic enablers—all possible pinch points. Populists and anti-immigrant politicians have worked for decades to roll out the ideological underpinnings of camps, slowly convincing a society that camps are necessary or normal. The inertial weight and momentum of the vast architecture, the billions in funding, and institutionalized harm all present a daunting challenge. If there is any lesson from Minneapolis and elsewhere it is this: We are up for that challenge.

And yet, as we have seen, the camp system cannot be shuttered—at least not permanently—through shutdown sprints, flickers, or even conflagrations of outrage. Rather, it takes years of slow, deliberate, careful, and caring community bonding. Dianey, neck-locked to the Adelanto gate, understood the stakes, and the urgency. She understood that while she had gained partial and provisional safety via DACA, her community and her family were still under systemic threat. She recognized that we are all bound up in each other, and that we must fight collectively, not just for ourselves and each other, but for our future.

We would do well to learn the lessons that Indigenous communities in struggle—the Yaqui pushing back the Spanish slavers in the sixteenth century, the American Indian Movement patrolling the streets of Minneapolis in the 1960s—have long been offering: Survival itself is a form of sacred resistance. Such generational and inclusive inheritance is key to the resilience necessary to shut down the camps. We survive and resist together.

ACKNOWLEDGMENTS

Given the urgency of the immigration crackdown and the rapid expansion of the camp system, Haymarket wanted a book detailing what was happening with immigration detention and how communities were responding—and they wanted it fast. We began discussing the project in the summer of 2025, and by late summer I had signed a contract. If we wanted the book out by 2026, I only had five months to research and write the thing. With a full-time reporting job and a young son, plus that niggling need to sleep, it was going to be a crunch. That's why I decided to take a slightly different, and more communal, approach to the book. I put a callout in my newsletter, not only for tips and suggestions but for people who might be interested in doing research or being first readers. I leaned into a community I already had, and met some wonderful new people who contributed, supported, researched, and refined what this book became. I particularly want to thank Shay Cohen-Jones, a great research intern I'd worked with in the past and who really stepped up to do some fabulous digging and generous/multiple reads of the sections on the Adelanto Camp. Adam Lewis plumbed history, especially of the internment era, and gave me the great rec on C. L. R. James, among a host of other additions. Max Granger helped put together the list of "A camp is . . ." examples and did an early read of a chapter. Colleen Falconer did another first read—really a first in-depth edit—of another tricky chapter. Yana Kunichoff gave some great recs on the intro. And so did my mentor and dear friend, John Granger. (There's not a sentence I write that hasn't been guided by him.) Tanvi Misra, a fabulous investigative reporter and friend, took a close first pass on a first draft of an initial chapter. Sebastian made some really astute edits on the conclusion and was a consistently helpful source of both news and clarity. Andrew Free helped with brainstorming sessions and lessons in how the system works—he's been a stalwart. Juan Castillo, who survived decades in prison and more than five years in the Etowah camp, was a frequent consultant and remains a polestar in my understanding of the reality and effects of the camps. Nina Douglass offered some great contacts and insights.

Silky Shah was the first person I talked to (outside of publishers and family) about the book, and she helped set the course and tenor. Her own book, *Unbuild Walls*, was a key inspiration and resource. Fred Tsao was generous to discuss at length about his history fighting, and so often winning, against the camps. Johannes Favi offered help, tips, and moral clarity. I was also given direction, tips, quotes, spirit, and support from Alejo, David Bennion, Ashley Hernandez, Marcela Hernandez, Bob Libal, Chris Lopez, Julie Macuga, Evy McDonald, Christopher W. McVoy, the folks of No Desert Data Center Coalition (especially Vivek Bharathan), Rosa and Lucia from La Ristra, Esmie T., Leif Taranta, Panagioti Tsolkas, and certainly others I am shamefully neglecting to name. Thank you. My former *Arizona Luminaria* colleagues Rafael Carranza, Shannon Conner,

Carolina Cuellar, Chelsea Curtis, and Yana Kunichoff gave me much-needed support during a particularly stressful professional stretch—thank you for the incredible work you do and the spirit you put into it.

I leaned again, as I did with my last book, into the camaraderie, friendship, and some past coreporting of José Olivarez. Bill Rogers and Marcia Levering, both former guards in Leavenworth, shared intimate stories and reflections about their experience. Josh Dunlap first recommended to me the David Graeber essay, which I read and reread. I also was the lucky recipient of support, expertise, wisdom, and *ánimo* of Nora Ahmed, Kenia Alcocer, Francisco Cantu, Ryan Deveraux, Jeff Migliozzi, Juan Ortiz, Leonardo Vilchis, and so many others. Ian Philabaum and Ariel Prado offered the questions and so much expertise and experience for the chapter on Torrance. Rebecca Sheff also provided a dose of clarity on how to move beyond the camp. My dear friend Gus Coliadis shared his story and has always been there and always will be for me. Nic Maier found and shared peace through the violence he confronted—his art and his way guides me. Thanks to Russ McSpadden, for his friendship and poetry and life poetics; Randy Serraglio, for sharing *The Nation* story about Danish resistance, and for his radical gift of gab; Andy Hsiao, for being that literary rock; Sean and Val for use of their space and the love to power me through crunch times; Joel Smith for brilliant brainstorming and systems thinking—and that deep care; Adam and Claire for generously opening their home in Patagonia; Emmett for lubricatory wine and a mushroom coffee; Aura Bogado for being a rock with sizzling brilliance; Geena Jackson for some school pickups and meals, as well as the courage she brings to daily life; and Kate and Miguel for stepping up, the moral support, and the radical sweetness.

Thanks to my agent and friend Roisin Davis, along with Anthony Arnove; editor Katy O'Donnell, for first bugging me about this book, for the idea, the support, and the fast and excellent editing. The Robert B. Silvers Foundation gave critical financial support through their Works in Progress grant.

Thanks to my animal cohabitants Tamarindo and the lovely sisters Virginia and Babette.

Thanks to my family, so deeply: my sister for her bottomless love and presence, Marko for the constructive conversations and hospitality, my mother and father for everything (more than I can ever thank them for), and my grandparents, especially Helen Blebea, the strongest person I've ever known.

All of that, and all of you, are in these pages.

And thank you—for it all, for the you and the presence and the spirit of love and goodness—Daniela and Elías.

APPENDIX 1

WHAT IT TAKES FOR A CAMP TO EXIST

MAPPING A PAPER TRAIL

Let us examine an example of some of the work that goes into building a camp. Researching the Adelanto ICE Processing Center, a camp about an hour and a half outside of Los Angeles, reveals a many-layered and wide-reaching bureaucracy of approval, acquiescence, and active allegiance. The hundreds of actors who signed, stamped, certified, licensed, voted for, financed, or took part in—even in minor form—construction, operation, and maintenance all bear responsibility. The following is meant to illustrate not only the myriad steps needed for a camp to be built but also the corresponding number of choke points. One single councilmember, contractor, inspector, or landscaper voting no or refusing service will not block a camp, but enough of them taking a stand together will.

1. Land and Facility Purchase and Transfer

On August 12, 2009, Adelanto City Manager James Hart signed a purchase and sale agreement with GEO Group, triggering a thirty-day public hearing. In early 2010, GEO Group paid $28 million to buy the Adelanto Community Correctional Facility, a 650-bed prison at the northeast corner of Raccoon Avenue and Rancho Road. The people locked up in the prison were transferred to other prisons, and the facility closed for a period of time after purchase. The city engineer, Wilson F. So, signed a certificate of compliance. In 2011, the City of Adelanto entered into an intergovernmental service agreement with ICE, and GEO subsequently contracted with the city to start locking up migrants.

- In 2011, GEO Group began building a 650-bed facility, with construction completed in late July of that year, costing $70 million. This brought the total number of beds to 1,300.
- City sale signed by city manager
- Certificate of compliance signed by city engineer

2. Zoning, Land Use, and Permitting

To use industrially zoned land as a detention center, GEO required a conditional use permit and a location and development plan, plus an array of linked permits: grading, building, vegetation removal, lot merger, and signage. Each of the following departments had to sign off on the plans:

- Planning Department – zoning, landscaping, verification of compliance
- City engineer – grading, storm drainage, mitigation, certification of completion
- Public Works Department – infrastructure, lighting, curbs, collection system
- Fire Department – fire code, water systems, hazardous materials

- Building Department – building permits, parking spaces
- County recorder – lot merger
- Environmental Health Department – abandoned well destruction
- Mojave Desert Air Quality Management District – air quality permit

3. Environmental Review

The California Environmental Quality Act (CEQA) required an Initial Study as part of the "Mitigated Negative Declaration and Mitigation Monitoring and Reporting Program" (2009), with a thirty-day public comment period and a hearing before the Planning Commission. The environmental review required an air quality and climate change impact analysis, a biological resource assessment, a traffic impact analysis, and a geotechnical evaluation. State agencies involved with the review included:

- California Department of Fish and Wildlife (CDFW)
- California Department of Forestry and Fire Protection (CAL FIRE)
- California Department of Parks and Recreation
- California Department of Transportation (Caltrans)
- California Department of Water Resources (DWR)
- California Energy Commission
- California Environmental Protection Agency (CalEPA)
- California Natural Resources Agency
- California Public Utilities Commission (CPUC)

- California State Lands Commission
- CalRecycle (Department of Resources Recycling and Recovery)
- Department of Conservation
- Department of Toxic Substances Control (DTSC)
- Native American Heritage Commission (NAHC)*
- State Water Resources Control Board

GEO Group applied for Conditional Use Permit (CUP) 09-04, Location and Development Plan (LDP) 09-02, along with the Mitigated Negative Declaration 09-05 to allow construction of a 2,200-bed detention/correctional facility.

4. Consultants, Surveyors, and Specialists

Private firms prepared environmental, traffic, biological, and geological reports. These included Flores Lund Consultants, MACTEC Engineering, Urban Crossroads, Circle Mountain Biological, Ninyo & Moore, and surveyors Douglas R. Melchior and Mike Radakovich. The final development agreement was completed in 2009.

5. Development Agreement and City Council Approval

The City Council approved the development agreement on October 14, 2009, after public hearings, declaring the facility consistent with the city's General Plan—signed by city manager, city clerk, city attorney, and GEO representatives.

---

* The chairman of the San Fernando Band of Mission Indians requested that a Native American monitor be present during project construction.

6. Services and Utilities

Electricity from Southern California Edison; water and sewer from Adelanto Public Utility Water District; gas and telecom from Southwest Gas, Time Warner, Verizon. Fire and water service letters required from city and county departments.

7. Federal and Local Contracts

GEO Group contracted with the City (May 17, 2011), followed by an ICE–City intergovernmental service agreement (IGSA) (May 27, 2011), allowing GEO to be paid $112 per detainee per day. Contracts enabled ICE to bypass procurement rules.

8. Permits

Permits were approved two years before Adelanto became an immigration detention camp and required other permits, reviewed and approved by city and state officials, including:

- Grading permits
- Native vegetation removal permit
- Land disturbance permit
- Lot merger application
- Building permits
- City encroachment permit (may or may not have been necessary)
- Separate approval for signage
- National Pollutant Discharge Elimination System general permit, as directed by California Water Resources Control Board, approved by Public Works Department

9. Licenses and Accreditations

Business licenses were required from city and state. GEO received accreditation from the American Correctional Association and National Commission on Correctional Health Care. In 2025, the American Correctional Association gave the camp a score of 99.6 percent.

10. Inspections and Enforcement Layers

Multiple inspection regimes overlapped, including the DHS Office of Inspector General, the Environmental Protection Agency, and later the Office of the Immigration Detention Ombudsman inspections, as well as a federal court order.

11. Renewals, Amendments, and Terminations

The original IGSA was terminated in 2019 after California passed AB32, a law that "bans" for-profit prisons and detention centers; ICE later signed a fifteen-year sole-source contract directly with GEO, extended through 2029. Local governments retain leverage via land use and permit renewals.

12. Each of These People Could Have Said No

None of this is inevitable. None of it is necessary.

APPENDIX 2

KNOW YOUR RIGHTS

Your rights on paper:

- *If you are a US citizen or have lawful immigration status and ICE stops you*: You can tell them your status and then ask them if you are free to go. If you are over eighteen and not a citizen, you're legally required to carry your "alien registration" papers with you at all times.
- *If you're undocumented*: You have the right to remain silent and don't have to discuss your immigration or citizenship status. Anything you tell an officer can be used against you if the government tries to deport you. ICE can't search your belongings without your consent, and you don't have to give it. You can carry a know-your-rights card—commonly known as red cards, or *tarjetas rojas*—and hand that to the officer in lieu of answering verbally. Red cards are available to download and print from the Immigrant Legal Resource Center: https://www.ilrc.org/red-cards.

- *If an officer knocks on your door*: Don't open it. Teach your children—and your children's friends, neighbors, aunts, and uncles—not to open the door. Officers must have a warrant signed by a judge (a judicial warrant) to enter your home, unless they're in "hot pursuit." ICE warrants aren't signed by judges; they are ICE forms signed by ICE officers, and they don't grant authority to enter a home without consent.
- *Don't sign any papers!*
- *Beware of ICE lies or ruses.* They may say they're investigating a crime, need your help, are protecting your child, but beware and be cautious.

How to Protect Yourself

Be prepared, have a plan:

- If you have children, identify responsible adults to take care of them if need be; consider identifying a temporary guardian.
- You may want to establish power of attorney, and to plan how you will continue to pay your mortgage, utility bills, and car or loan payments if you're arrested.
- Keep all your documents, including medical records, in a safe place where they will be accessible to someone you trust.
- Consider singing a G28 form to be represented by an attorney and an ICE 60-001 form, which authorizes third-party disclosure about your case. Those documents can be essential to accessing legal

representation and getting your story (and hopefully you) out.

- Get to know your neighbors! Say hello, knock on their doors, offer a dish of food or to water some plants. Make a plan with them in case ICE comes prowling. The strongest weapon against ICE, and against the camp, is a tightly bonded community.

APPENDIX 3

PUBLIC RECORDS AND DISSECTING THE CAMP

Public Records Requests

Adapt the records request language below for your state and city/county records law; make use of the Freedom of Information Act (FOIA) for federal records. Search who grants licenses and permits, and start requesting the records.

- "All current licenses held by [camp name], including application, renewal, and inspection records."
- "All building, occupancy, and zoning permits for [camp address]."
- "All contracts between [county/city] and ICE, GEO Group, CoreCivic, or any other detention facility operator."
- "All inspection reports, violation notices, and corrective action plans for [facility name] from [date] to present."

Questions to Ask of a Camp

The following questions about camps are meant to serve as a framework, a checklist, and a provocation. These questions aim to open lines of investigation into how immigrant incarceration functions, who profits from it, and how power and responsibility are distributed. Collectively, these questions can expose some of the hidden architecture of detention—and the points at which it may be most vulnerable to challenge and closure. The questions were first developed by the team at Innovation Law Lab.

I. Detained Population

Custody and capacity

- What is the total capacity (bed space) of the facility?
- Which agencies have held or currently hold custody of detained people?
  - *ICE*: Currently? If so, since when? Formerly—if so, when?
  - *US Marshals Service*: Currently? Since when? Formerly—when?
  - *State corrections*: Currently? Since when? Formerly—when?
  - *County jail system*: Currently? Since when? Formerly—when?
  - *Other federal agencies*: Currently? Since when? Formerly—when?

Contracting authority

- Who signed the current operating contract?
- Are there previous contracts or amendments? Who signed those?

II. Oversight and Inspections

Regulatory inspections

- Is there a comprehensive list of inspections and accreditations required for operation?
- Which agencies conduct annual inspections?
  - Municipal
  - County
  - State
  - Federal

Auditing and accreditation

- Which entities conduct audits or compliance reviews?
- What mechanisms exist for revoking accreditation or certification?
- What alternatives exist if accreditation is revoked?

III. Medical and Mental Health Services

Internal medical services

- What is the name of the medical services provider?
  - Who do they contract with?
  - Is the contract publicly accessible?
  - Do they subcontract any services?
  - Who provides HIPAA oversight?

- What accreditations apply (e.g., National Commission on Correctional Health Care)?
- Who conducts audits and ensures accountability?
- Who is responsible for harm caused by malpractice, negligence, or systemic failures?

Mental and dental health services

- Mental health:
    - Name of provider
    - Contracting details, accreditation, and audit procedures
- Dental health:
    - Name of provider
    - Contracting details, accreditation, and audit procedures

External medical services

- Is there an agreement with outside providers for services unavailable onsite?
- Can records from external providers be obtained?
- Who is liable for harm if external recommendations are ignored?
- Are external providers responsible for due diligence or follow-up?

Documentation and accountability

- What is the operator's level of access to detainee medical records?
- How is that access established (e.g., signed consent forms)?

- What potential HIPAA violations may occur, and what recourse exists (grievance, litigation, accountability)?

Costs

- How much does ICE spend annually on healthcare at this facility?

IV. Labor by Detained People

- Is the facility subject to state labor laws?
    - What is the state minimum wage?
    - Can the operator be compelled to pay minimum wage to detained workers?
- What authority does OSHA have to regulate or penalize unsafe or exploitative conditions?
    - Can OSHA suspend operations or initiate investigations?
- What are the policies on breaks, safety, and workplace hazards?
- Are local or state authorities liable if detained people perform labor under this contract?

V. Food Services

- Who provides food and kitchen services?
- Who conducts kitchen and health inspections? Are records available?
- Who holds food-handling licenses?
    - Is a licensed supervisor present at all times?
    - Are detained workers trained or licensed in food handling?

VI. Infrastructure and Environment

Buildings

- When was the facility built, and what was its estimated lifespan?
- What infrastructure is required for operation (plumbing, sewage, electrical, water, etc.)?
- Who conducts building and systems inspections?
    - Safety
    - Plumbing
    - Electrical
    - Sewage
    - Water and utilities

Water and sewage

- Who is responsible for plumbing and water systems?
- What issues exist with plumbing, sewage, or water quality?
- Is there a separate sewage contract?

VII. Transportation

- Who provides transportation for people in custody?
- Who accredits or regulates transportation operations?
- What standards or regulations govern these contracts?

VIII. Commissary

- Which company operates the commissary?
- Who sets prices, and how are they monitored or regulated?

IX. Land, Location, and Local Constituencies

Geographic and historical context

- What is the regional and Indigenous history of the land?
- What do US Geological Survey or other maps reveal about the site and its surroundings?

Property data

- Parcel number and assessor's map link
- Current property owner and classification (e.g., nonresidential)
- Recent tax and assessment history
- Are there environmental or public health implications linked to property classification or usage?

X. Staff and Operations

Workforce and unionization

- Authorized vs. actual staffing levels
- Local vs. temporary-duty staff numbers
- Is there a staff union?
  - Local or shop leadership
  - Camp stewards
  - Collective bargaining agreement
  - Regional contact information

Leadership

- Warden
- Assistant warden
- Warden's secretary
- Visitation and counselor supervisors

ICE officials

- Field office director (FOD)
- Deputy and assistant FODs
- Supervisory and regular deportation officers (SDDOs, DOs)
- ICE liaison(s)

Other authorities

- State officials
- County commissioners
- Municipal authorities

XI. Private Camp Operator

- Company name and headquarters location
- Business information and ownership structure
- SEC filings and shareholder reports
- Annual 10-K filings

XII. Oversight, Leverage, and Accountability

- What auditing or oversight mechanisms could be used to pressure contract termination?
- What factors might motivate officials or operators to end the contract (financial, reputational, legal, or political)?
- Has the facility ever shut down before?
    - If yes, why, and what can be learned from that closure?
- What public records requests can be filed?

- Communications between public entities and the private operator
- Communications between public entities and ICE
- 911 calls or incident reports

APPENDIX 4

ADDITIONAL RESOURCES

Detention Watch Network (particularly DWN's "Communities Not Cages" campaign), Immigrant Legal Resource Center, as well as other organizations offer a wealth of resources to protect community members and push back against camps. A few minutes of online searching will typically turn up nearby local organizations already doing great work. Go to the Haymarket Books website (www.haymarketbooks.org/books/2880-how-to-close-a-camp) to see these and more resources.

Know Your Rights and Practical Tools

Know-your-rights guides

- American Civil Liberties Union – Immigrants' Rights: Know Your Rights: https://www.aclu.org/know-your-rights/immigrants-rights
- Immigrant Legal Resource Center – Know Your Rights Toolkit: https://www.ilrc.org/resources/community/know-your-rights-toolkit
- Immigration scholar Austin Kocher has collected a voluminous list of know-your-rights information

for individuals and employers, including what to do and where to read more about a wide variety of situations. Learn more: https://austinkocher.substack.com/p/know-your-rights-resources-for-ice.

Printable rights cards

- Immigrant Legal Resource Center – Red Cards (Tarjetas Rojas) (wallet-sized cards in multiple languages to assert rights during ICE encounters): https://www.ilrc.org/red-cards

Organizing and Research

- Deportation Data Project: https://deportationdata.org/data.html
- Detention Watch Network: https://www.detentionwatchnetwork.org/
- League of United Latin American Citizens – El Escudo: Immigrant Rights and Resources Toolkit: https://lulac.org/know_your_rights/
- Legal Aid Justice Center – Rapid Response Toolkit: https://www.justice4all.org/rapid-response-toolkit/
- Immigrant Defense Project: https://www.immigrantdefenseproject.org/raids-toolkit/
- International Detention Coalition: https://idcoalition.org/
- Transactional Records Access Clearinghouse: https://tracreports.org/immigration/

Immigration Policy News and Analysis

- *The Border Chronicle* (news, analysis, interviews): https://www.theborderchronicle.com/
- Andrew Free, *#Detention Kills* (newsletter on deaths in detention and tools for immigration research): https://detentionkills.substack.com/
- Kelly Hayes, *Movement Memos* (podcast with activists and journalists about movement work and mutual aid): https://truthout.org/series/movement-memos/
- César Cuauhtémoc García Hernández, *Immigration Law Unhinged* (Substack newsletter on law, policy, and detention): https://ccgarciahernandez.com/
- Austin Kocher, *Immigration Enforcement and Data* (newsletter with detailed analysis of detention trends, ICE data, and enforcement infrastructure): https://austinkocher.substack.com/
- Kate Morrissey, *Beyond the Border* (newsletter on immigration policy and weekly recaps): https://beyondthebordernews.substack.com/
- John Washington, *Lit and Border News* (newsletter of reflections on border and literature): https://johnwashington.substack.com/

Books

- Kelly Lytle Hernández, *Migra! A History of the US Border Patrol*, University of California Press, 2010.
- Reece Jones, *Violent Borders: Refugees and the Right to Move*, Verso, 2017.

- César Cuauhtémoc García Hernández, *Migrating to Prison: America's Obsession with Locking Up Immigrants*, The New Press, 2019.
- Todd Miller, *Empire of Borders: The Expansion of the US Border Around the World*, Verso, 2019.
- Greg Grandin, *The End of the Myth: From the Frontier to the Border Wall in the Mind of America*, Metropolitan Books, 2020.
- Harsha Walia, *Border and Rule: Global Migration, Capitalism, and the Rise of Racist Nationalism*, Haymarket Books, 2021.
- Michelle Castañeda, *Disappearing Rooms: The Hidden Theaters of Immigration Law,* Duke University Press, 2023.
- Joseph Carens, *The Ethics of Immigration*, Oxford University Press, 2023.
- Silky Shah, *Unbuild Walls: Why Immigrant Justice Needs Abolition*, Haymarket Books, 2024.
- Jonathan Blitzer, *Everyone Who Is Gone Is Here: Seeking Sanctuary in America*, Penguin Press, 2025.
- Nancy Hiemstra and Deirdre Conlon, *Immigration Detention Inc.: The Big Business of Locking up Migrants*, Pluto Press, 2025.

NOTES

Introduction

1. Adriana Gomez Licon and Will Weissert, "Trump Tours Florida Immigration Lockup," *AP News*, July 1, 2025, https://apnews.com/article/trump-everglades-immigrant-detention-facility-visit-5dc5568ec15534947c29c9149b773d1d.
2. Churchill Ndonwie, "FEMA Will Give $608 Million to States for Migrant Detention Facilities," *Miami Herald*, July 28, 2025, https://www.governing.com/infrastructure/fema-will-give-608-million-to-states-for-migrant-detention-facilities.
3. NOAA National Centers for Environmental Information, "U.S. Billion-Dollar Weather and Climate Disasters: Florida State Summary," 2025, accessed March 29, 2026, https://www.ncei.noaa.gov/access/billions/state-summary/FL.
4. Abel Fernández, "The Mysterious Disappearance of Hundreds of Immigrants Detained at Alligator Alcatraz," *El País English*, September 18, 2025, https://english.elpais.com/usa/2025-09-18/the-mysterious-disappearance-of-hundreds-of-immigrants-detained-at-alligator-alcatraz.html.
5. C.M.V. v. Noem, 1:25-cv-23182 (S.D. Flo. 2025).
6. *Torture and Enforced Disappearances in the Sunshine State: Human Rights Violations at "Alligator Alcatraz" and Krome in Florida*, AMR 51/0511/2025 (Amnesty International Netherlands, December 2025), https://www.amnesty.nl/content/uploads/2025/12/AMR_51_0511_2025-Torture-

and-enforced-disappearances-in-the-Sunshine-State-vf.pdf.

7. Associated Press, "Trump Announces 'Border Czar' Will Be Tom Homan, Former Head of Immigration Enforcement," CBS News, November 11, 2024, https://www.cbsnews.com/news/trump-border-czar-tom-homan-former-immigration-enforcement-head/.
8. Juan Castillo, Etowah County Detention Center, Alabama, 2022. John Washington, "The Elusive Freedom of Juan Castillo," *Latino USA*, podcast, January 14, 2022, https://www.latinousa.org/2022/01/14/juancastillo/.
9. Unnamed child and mother, Artesia Family Residential Center, New Mexico, 2018. Scott Allen and Pamela McPherson, DHS Office for Civil Rights and Civil Liberties, to Senators Charles E. Grassley and Ron Wyden, July 17, 2018, https://www.wyden.senate.gov/imo/media/doc/Doctors%20Congressional%20Disclosure%20SWC.pdf.
10. Jesús Manuel Galindo, Reeves County Detention Center, Texas, 2008. "ACLU of Texas Sues on Behalf of Immigrant Inmate Who Died in Solitary Confinement in Pecos Prison," press release, ACLU of Texas, December 8, 2010, https://www.aclutx.org/en/press-releases/aclu-texas-sues-behalf-immigrant-inmate-who-died-solitary-confinement-pecos-prison.
11. Andry Hernández Romero, Terrorism Confinement Center (CECOT), El Salvador, 2025. Andrea Castillo, "'Is Being Gay a Crime?' Venezuelan Makeup Artist Rebuilds Life After 125 Days in El Salvador Prison," *Los Angeles Times*, September 11, 2025, https://www.latimes.com/politics/story/2025-09-11/gay-venezuelan-makeup-artist-detained-in-san-diego-and-sent-to-el-salvador-prison-rebuilds-life.
12. Brianna Nofil, *The Deportation Machine: America's Long History of Expelling Immigrants* (Princeton, NJ: Princeton University Press, 2020).
13. Kelly Lytle Hernández, *City of Inmates: Conquest, Rebellion,*

and the Rise of Human Caging in Los Angeles, 1771–1965 (Chapel Hill: University of North Carolina Press, 2017).

14. James Baldwin, "The Fire Next Time," in *The Fire Next Time* (New York: Dial Press, 1963).
15. The White House, "Protecting the American People Against Invasion," January 20, 2025, https://www.whitehouse.gov/presidential-actions/2025/01/protecting-the-american-people-against-invasion/.
16. US Department of Homeland Security, Immigration and Customs Enforcement, "Class Urgent and Compelling Justification for Multiple Detention Facilities Supporting ICE," Contract Award Nos. 70CDCR25D00000008, 70CDCR25D00000009, 70CDCR25D00000010, SAM.gov, March 7, 2025, https://sam.gov/opp/e9aa4c41a123404fbfa22773026cdc99/view.
17. John Feng and Brendan Cole, "ICE Budget Now Bigger Than Most of the World's Militaries," *Newsweek*, July 2, 2025, https://www.newsweek.com/immigration-ice-bill-trump-2093456.
18. Judd Legum, "ICE Boosts Weapons Spending 700%," Popular Information, October 20, 2025, https://popular.info/p/ice-boosts-weapons-spending-700.
19. Joshua Kaplan et al., "Kristi Noem–Tied Firm Secretly Got Piece of $220 Million DHS Ad Campaign," *ProPublica*, November 14, 2025, https://www.propublica.org/article/kristi-noem-dhs-ad-campaign-strategy-group.
20. Avery Lotz, "A Disturbance in the Force: White House Star Wars Day Post Raises Eyebrows," *Axios*, May 4, 2025, https://www.axios.com/2025/05/04/trump-white-house-star-wars-post; Department of Homeland Security (@DHSgov), "The peace of a nation no longer besieged by the third world," X (formerly Twitter), May 5, 2025, https://x.com/DHSgov/status/2006472108222853298.

21. Michael Waldman, "Big Budget Act Creates Deportation Industrial Complex," Brennan Center for Justice, July 3, 2025, https://www.brennancenter.org/our-work/analysis-opinion/big-budget-act-creates-deportation-industrial-complex.
22. State of New Hampshire, Office of the Governor, "ICE Detention Reengineering Initiative," n.d., https://www.governor.nh.gov/sites/g/files/ehbemt971/files/inline-documents/merrimack-detention-reengineering-initiative.pdf.
23. Mica Rosenberg et al., "ICE Sent 600 Immigrant Kids to Detention in Federal Shelters This Year. It's a New Record," *ProPublica*, November 24, 2025, https://www.propublica.org/article/ice-detentions-immigrant-kids-family-separations.
24. Jeff Ernsthausen et al., "Trump Has Detained the Parents of More Than 11,000 U.S. Citizen Kids," *ProPublica*, March 23, 2026, https://www.propublica.org/article/trump-family-deportations-ice-citizen-kids.
25. Natasha Bertrand and Priscilla Alvarez, "Trump Administration Turns to the U.S. Navy to Build Migrant Detention Centers," CNN, October 24, 2025, https://www.cnn.com/2025/10/24/politics/navy-building-ice-detention-facilities.
26. Julia Ainsley and David Ingram, "'Mega Detention Centers': ICE Considers Buying Large Warehouses to Hold Immigrants," NBC, November 7, 2025, https://www.nbcnews.com/politics/immigration/mega-detention-centers-ice-considers-buying-large-warehouses-hold-immi-rcna242423.
27. *Immigration Detention Expansion in Trump's Second Term* (American Immigration Council, January 14, 2026), https://www.americanimmigrationcouncil.org/report/immigration-detention/.
28. Associated Press, "Watch: Stephen Miller Says Trump Administration Is 'Actively Looking At' Suspending Habeas Corpus," *PBS NewsHour*, May 9, 2025, https://www.pbs.org/newshour/politics/watch-stephen-miller-says-trump-admin-

istration-is-actively-looking-at-suspending-habeas-corpus.

29. Politico, "Immigration Appeals Court Expands Mandatory Detention for Millions," September 5, 2025, https://www.politico.com/news/2025/09/05/immigration-mandatory-detention-00548660.
30. *Torture and Enforced Disappearances in the Sunshine State: Human Rights Violations at "Alligator Alcatraz" and Krome in Florida* (Amnesty International, 2025), https://www.amnestyusa.org/wp-content/uploads/2025/12/Torture-and-Enforced-Disappearances-in-the-Sunshine-State-Human-Rights-Violations-at-Alligator-Alcatraz-and-Krome-in-Florida.pdf.
31. *Immigration Detention Expansion in Trump's Second Term* (American Immigration Council, January 2026), https://www.americanimmigrationcouncil.org/report/immigration-detention/.
32. Nicole Foy, "We Found That More than 170 U.S. Citizens Have Been Held by Immigration Agents. They've Been Kicked, Dragged and Detained for Days," *ProPublica*, October 16, 2025, https://www.propublica.org/article/immigration-dhs-american-citizens-arrested-detained-against-will.
33. "Dexter Highlights Human Toll of Trump's Immigration Machine; Elevates Merlos Family's Story on Capitol Hill," press release, Congresswoman Maxine Dexter, September 19, 2025, https://dexter.house.gov/media/press-releases/dexter-highlights-human-toll-trumps-immigration-machine-elevates-merlos.
34. Jonah E. Bromwich, "ICE Agents Menaced Minnesota Protesters at Their Homes, Filings Say," *New York Times*, February 13, 2026, https://www.nytimes.com/2026/02/13/us/minneapolis-ice-agents-protester-home-visits.html; Drew Harwell and Joyce Sohyun Lee, "ICE Plans $100 Million Recruitment Push Targeting Gun Shows, Military Fans,"

Washington Post, December 31, 2025, https://www.washingtonpost.com/technology/2025/12/31/ice-wartime-recruitment-push/.

35. Nick Miroff, "Fast Times at Immigration and Customs Enforcement," *The Atlantic*, August 26, 2025, https://www.theatlantic.com/politics/archive/2025/08/ice-recruitment-immigration-enforcement-billions/684000/.
36. Jermaine Fowler, "ICE Are the New Proud Boys," *The Humanity Archive* (Substack), November 10, 2025, https://thehumanityarchive.substack.com/p/ice-are-the-new-proud-boys.
37. Allison McCann et al., "Trump Administration Aims to Spend $45 Billion to Expand Immigrant Detention Facilities and Services," *New York Times*, April 7, 2025, https://www.nytimes.com/2025/04/07/us/politics/trump-administration-immigrant-detention-facilities-services.html.
38. Katherine Culliton-Gonzalez and Lama Elsharif, *Trump's Budget Bill Benefits Private Immigration Detention Companies That Donated to Trump* (Citizens for Responsibility and Ethics in Washington, July 23, 2025), https://www.citizensforethics.org/reports-investigations/crew-investigations/trumps-budget-bill-benefits-private-immigration-detention-companies-that-donated-to-trump/.
39. Nick Schwellenbach and René Kladzyk, "Private Prison Giant Hired ICE Detention Chief," Project on Government Oversight, January 17, 2025, https://www.pogo.org/investigates/private-prison-giant-hired-ice-detention-chief.
40. Carol Leonnig and Ken Dilanian, "Tom Homan Was Investigated for Accepting $50,000 from Undercover FBI Agents. Trump's DOJ Shut It Down," MSNBC, September 20, 2025, https://www.msnbc.com/msnbc/news/tom-homan-cash-contracts-trump-doj-investigation-rcna232568.
41. Jesse Bogan, "Trump's Vow to Arrest Immigrants Lifted Private Prison Stocks. Then Why Did They Tank?," *The Marshall*

Project, January 6, 2026, https://www.themarshallproject.org/2026/01/06/trump-arrest-immigrants-private-prisons.

42. César Cuauhtémoc García Hernández, *Migrating to Prison: America's Obsession with Locking Up Immigrants* (New York: The New Press, 2019).
43. Douglas MacMillan et al., "ICE Documents Reveal Plan to Double Immigrant Detention Space This Year," *Washington Post*, August 15, 2025, https://www.washingtonpost.com/immigration/2025/08/15/ice-documents-reveal-plan-double-immigrant-detention-space-this-year/.
44. Kathryn Palmer, "Trump Says ICE Raids 'Haven't Gone Far Enough' in 60 Minutes Interview," *USA Today*, November 3, 2025, https://www.usatoday.com/story/news/politics/2025/11/03/trump-ice-raids-60-minutes-interview/87062540007/.
45. Michelle Castañeda, *Disappearing Rooms: The Hidden Theaters of Immigration Law* (Durham, NC: Duke University Press, 2023).
46. Jonathan Chait, "Stephen Miller's Charlie Kirk Funeral," *The Atlantic*, September 22, 2025, https://www.theatlantic.com/politics/archive/2025/09/stephen-millers-charlie-kirk-funeral/684301/.
47. Giorgio Agamben, *Homo Sacer: Sovereign Power and Bare Life*, trans. Daniel Heller-Roazen (Stanford: Stanford University Press, 1998).
48. Dan Stone, *Concentration Camps: A Very Short Introduction* (New York: Oxford University Press, 2019).
49. Kathleen DuVal, *Native Nations: A Millennium in North America* (New York: Random House, 2024).
50. Thomas Jefferson to George Rogers Clark, January 1, 1780, Founders Online, National Archives, https://founders.archives.gov/documents/Jefferson/01-03-02-0289. Originally published in *The Papers of Thomas Jefferson*, vol. 3, *18*

June 1779–30 September 1780, ed. Julian P. Boyd (Princeton: Princeton University Press, 1951).

51. DuVal, *Native Nations.*
52. Mahmood Mamdani, *Neither Settler nor Native: The Making and Unmaking of Permanent Minorities* (Cambridge, MA: Harvard University Press, 2020).
53. Agamben, *Homo Sacer.*
54. Marco Rubio, "Secretary of State Marco Rubio at the Munich Security Conference" (speech, Munich Security Conference, Hotel Bayerischer Hof, Munich, Germany, February 14, 2026), US Department of State, https://www.state.gov/releases/office-of-the-spokesperson/2026/02/secretary-of-state-marco-rubio-at-the-munich-security-conference.
55. Christophe Bident, *Maurice Blanchot: A Critical Biography*, trans. John McKeane (New York: Fordham University Press, 2019).
56. Peter Beilharz, ed., *The Bauman Reader* (Malden, MA: Blackwell Publishers, 2001).
57. Austin Kocher, "Immigrant Detention by the Numbers: A Baseline for Evaluating ICE's Ramped-Up Enforcement Efforts," *Austin Kocher* (blog), January 24, 2025, https://austinkocher.substack.com/p/immigrant-detention-by-the-numbers.
58. Sarah Stillman, "Disappeared to a Foreign Prison," *New Yorker*, December 1, 2025, https://www.newyorker.com/magazine/2025/12/01/disappeared-to-a-foreign-prison.
59. Gary Paul Nabhan, *Against the American Grain: A Borderlands History of Resistance* (Oakland: University of California Press, 2025).
60. Thomas Nail, *Theory of the Border* (New York: Oxford University Press, 2016).
61. Lisa Lerer et al., "Can Democrats Find Their Way on Immigration?," *New York Times*, July 6, 2025, https://www.nytimes.com/2025/07/06/us/politics/democrats-immigration-trump.html.

62. Elliott Young, *Forever Prisoners: How the United States Made the World's Largest Immigrant Detention System* (New York: Oxford University Press, 2021).
63. Washington, "Elusive Freedom."
64. Greg Bailey, "Etowah Jail Gets Face Lift; ICE Detainees Returning," *Gadsden Times*, February 27, 2025, https://www.gadsdentimes.com/story/news/2025/02/27/etowah-jail-gets-face-lift-ice-detainees-returning/80138434007/.
65. Castañeda, *Disappearing Rooms.*
66. *Lessons from the ICE Detention Contract Termination in Contra Costa County, CA* (Interfaith Movement for Human Integrity, December 4, 2019), https://www.im4humanintegrity.org/2019/12/lessons-from-the-ice-detention-contract-termination-in-contra-costa-county-ca/.
67. *If You Build It, ICE Will Fill It: The Link Between Detention Capacity and ICE Arrests* (Immigrant Legal Resource Center; Detention Watch Network; CERES Policy Research, September 29, 2022), https://www.ilrc.org/resources/if-you-build-it-ice-will-fill-it-link-between-detention-capacity-and-ice-arrests.
68. Monserrath López, South Texas ICE Processing Center, Texas, 2014. See *"Do You See How Much I'm Suffering Here?" Abuse Against Transgender Women in US Immigration Detention* (Human Rights Watch, 2016), https://www.hrw.org/report/2016/03/23/do-you-see-how-much-im-suffering-here/abuse-against-transgender-women-us.
69. Unnamed man, Leavenworth Detention Center, Kansas, 2021. ACLU of Kansas, Missouri, Iowa, and Nebraska to White House Policy Counsel Office, September 2, 2021, https://www.aclukansas.org/app/uploads/2021/09/letter_regarding_corecivic_leavenworth_redacted.pdf.
70. Unnamed woman, Jackson County Correctional Facility, Florida, late 1990s. Nofil, *Deportation Machine.*

1. "Savage Exclusion": The History of the Camp

1. César Cuauhtémoc García Hernández, *Migrating to Prison: America's Obsession with Locking up Migrants* (New York: The New Press, 2019).
2. Hernández, *Migrating to Prison.*
3. Kelly Lytle Hernández, *City of Inmates: Conquest, Rebellion, and the Rise of Human Caging in Los Angeles, 1771–1965* (Chapel Hill: University of North Carolina Press, 2017).
4. An Act to Execute Certain Treaty Stipulations Relating to the Chinese (Chinese Exclusion Act), Pub. L. 47-126, 22 Stat. 58 (May 6, 1882), General Records of the United States Government, Record Group 11, National Archives, https://www.archives.gov/milestone-documents/chinese-exclusion-act.
5. Brianna Nofil, *The Migrant's Jail: An American History of Mass Incarceration* (Princeton: Princeton University Press, 2024).
6. Fong Yue Ting v. United States, 149 U.S. 698 (1893).
7. Plessy v. Ferguson, 163 U.S. 537 (1896).
8. Patrick Lohmann, "Sewage Flooding Cells Inside Torrance County ICE Prison Again, Advocates Say," *Source New Mexico*, May 2, 2025, https://sourcenm.com/2025/05/02/sewage-flooding-cells-inside-torrance-county-ice-prison-again-advocates-say/.
9. "Open Letter from 'Los Últimos Guerreros,' the Last People Detained by ICE at Torrance County Detention Facility," Innovation Law Lab, December 2022, https://innovationlawlab.org/resource/open-letter-los-ultimos-guerreros-last-people-detained-ice-torrance-county-detention.
10. *"You Feel Like Your Life Is Over": Abusive Practices at Three Florida Immigration Detention Centers Since January 2025* (Human Rights Watch, July 21, 2025), https://www.hrw.org/report/2025/07/21/you-feel-like-your-life-is-over/abusive-practices-at-three-florida-immigration.

11. Ruth Wilson Gilmore, *Golden Gulag: Prisons, Surplus, Crisis, and Opposition in Globalizing California* (Berkeley: University of California Press, 2007).
12. César Cuauhtémoc García Hernández, "Ellis Island Welcomed Thousands to America—But It Was Also a Detention Center," *Time*, January 1, 2020, https://www.yahoo.com/news/ellis-island-welcomed-thousands-america-160050974.html.
13. "Angel Island State Park: A Journey Through Immigration, Identity, and Belonging," *California State Parks Foundation Blog*, July 16, 2025, https://www.calparks.org/blog/angel-island-state-park-journey-through-immigration-identity-and-belonging.
14. "Angel Island Poetry," Facing History & Ourselves, updated January 27, 2023, https://www.facinghistory.org/resource-library/angel-island-poetry.
15. C. L. R. James, *Mariners, Renegades and Castaways: The Story of Herman Melville and the World We Live In* (1953; repr., Hanover, NH: University Press of New England, 2001).
16. Corey Robin, "Trump Is Building the Blue Scare," interview by Ezra Klein, *The Ezra Klein Show* (podcast), *New York Times*, September 24, 2025, https://www.nytimes.com/2025/09/24/opinion/ezra-klein-podcast-corey-robin.html.
17. Gary Y. Okihiro, ed., *Encyclopedia of Japanese American Internment* (Santa Barbara, CA: Greenwood, 2013).
18. Danielle Bainbridge, "Concentration Camps Are Older Than World War II," *Origin of Everything*, season 3, episode 12, PBS Digital Studios, June 11, 2020, https://www.pbs.org/video/concentration-camps-are-older-than-world-war-ii-pk9rcq/.
19. Brandon Shimoda, *The Afterlife Is Letting Go* (New York: Nightboat Books, 2024).
20. "Sold, Damaged, Stolen, Gone: Japanese American Property Loss During WWII," Densho, April 4, 2017, https://densho.org/catalyst/sold-damaged-stolen-gone-japanese-ameri-

can-property-loss-wwii/.

21. Quoted in Maddalena Marinari, "Divided and Conquered: Immigration Reform Advocates and the Passage of the 1952 Immigration and Nationality Act," *Journal of American Ethnic History* 35, no. 3 (Spring 2016): 9–40, https://doi.org/10.5406/jamerethnhist.35.3.0009.
22. "Text of U.S. Attorney General's Talk to New Citizens," *New York Times*, November 12, 1954, https://www.nytimes.com/1954/11/12/archives/text-of-us-attorney-generals-talk-to-new-citizens.html.
23. Jessica Ordaz, *The Shadow of El Centro: A History of Migrant Incarceration and Solidarity* (Chapel Hill: University of North Carolina Press, 2021).
24. Nofil, *Migrant's Jail.*
25. Mae M. Ngai, *Impossible Subjects: Illegal Aliens and the Making of Modern America* (Princeton, NJ: Princeton University Press, 2004).
26. "Immigration Reform Policy Papers," March 6, 1981 – November 29, 1982, Ronald Reagan Presidential Library and Museum, https://www.reaganlibrary.gov/public/documents/edwebdocs/Website.ImmigrationReform.PolicyPapers.pdf.
27. Kristina Shull, "'A Recession-Proof Industry': Reagan's Immigration Crisis and the Birth of the Neoliberal Security State," *Border Criminologies Blog*, University of Oxford, April 30, 2015, https://blogs.law.ox.ac.uk/research-subject-groups/centre-criminology/centreborder-criminologies/blog/2015/04/%E2%80%98-recession-proof.
28. *Communities Not Cages: A Just Transition from Immigration Detention Economies* (Washington, DC: Detention Watch Network, May 2021), https://www.detentionwatchnetwork.org/sites/default/files/reports/Communities%20Not%20Cages-A%20Just%20Transition%20from%20Immigration%20Detention%20Economies_DWN%202021.pdf.

29. US House of Representatives, Department of Homeland Security Appropriations Act, 2010, H. Rept. 111-298, 111th Cong., 1st sess. (October 13, 2009), https://www.congress.gov/committee-report/111th-congress/house-report/298.
30. Hannah Rappleye and Lisa Riordan Seville, "How One Georgia Town Gambled Its Future on Immigration Detention," *The Nation*, April 10, 2012, https://www.thenation.com/article/archive/how-one-georgia-town-gambled-its-future-immigration-detention/.
31. Hannah Rappleye and Lisa Riordan Seville, "Gambling on Immigration Detention," *The Nation*, April 11, 2012, https://www.typeinvestigations.org/investigation/2012/04/11/gambling-immigration-detention/.
32. Rappleye and Seville, "Gambling on Immigration Detention."
33. José Olivares and John Washington, "Number of Women Alleging Misconduct by ICE Gynecologist Nearly Triples," *The Intercept*, October 27, 2020, https://theintercept.com/2020/10/27/ice-irwin-women-hysterectomies-senate/.
34. Alejandro Serrano, "South Texas Immigration Detention Center with Capacity for 2,400 People to Reopen," *Texas Tribune*, March 6, 2025, https://www.texastribune.org/2025/03/06/texas-dilley-immigration-detention-center-families-reopen/.
35. Priscilla Alvarez and Michael Williams, "Exclusive: Migrant Families Paint Grim Picture of Life in Texas ICE Detention Facility, New Court Documents Show," CNN, December 9, 2025, https://www.cnn.com/2025/12/09/politics/migrant-families-ice-detention-facility-texas.
36. B. Useem and V. C. Kimball, *Resolution of Prison Riots*, NCJRS 147708 (Washington, DC: US Department of Justice, Office of Justice Programs, National Institute of Justice, 1993), https://www.ojp.gov/pdffiles1/Digitization/147708NCJRS.pdf.

37. Eduardo Cuevas and Lauren Villagran, "Army Base Used for WWII Japanese Internment Now Nation's Largest ICE Detention Center," *USA Today*, August 23, 2025, https://www.aol.com/army-used-wwii-japanese-internment-124435120.html.
38. "Army Base Used for WWII Japanese Internment Will Be Nation's Largest ICE Detention Center," *USA Today*, August 25, 2025, YouTube video, https://www.youtube.com/watch?v=OxzNHFEFchE.

2. The Toll of the Camp

1. Unnamed woman, Chula Vista Border Patrol Station, California, 2020. ACLU to Joseph V. Cuffari, DHS Office of Inspector General, April 8, 2020, available at https://embed.documentcloud.org/documents/6827805-2020-04-07-OIG-Cmplt-Final-Redacted/.
2. Unnamed man, Kingsville Border Patrol station, Texas, 2019. *"They Treat You Like You Are Worthless": Internal DHS Reports of Abuses by US Border Officials* (Human Rights Watch, October 21, 2021), https://www.hrw.org/report/2021/10/21/they-treat-you-you-are-worthless/internal-dhs-reports-abuses-us-border-officials.
3. Unnamed man, South Florida detention facility ("Alligator Alcatraz"), Florida, 2025. Richard Luscombe, "'Alligator Alcatraz' Detainees Face Abuse and Are Denied Due Process, Say Lawyers," *Guardian*, August 18, 2025, https://www.theguardian.com/us-news/2025/aug/18/alligator-alcatraz-lawsuit-abuse-immigration.
4. Unnamed woman, Irwin County Detention Center, Georgia, 2020. Seth Freed Wessler, "Fear, Illness and Death in ICE Detention: How a Protest Grew on the Inside," *New York Times*, June 4, 2020, https://www.nytimes.com/2020/06/04/magazine/covid-ice.html#:~:text=That%20same%20day%2C%20Manrique%20was,been%20tested%20for%20the%20virus.

5. Lead Compliance Inspector, The Nakamoto Group, to Assistant Director for Detention Management, US Immigration and Customs Enforcement, February 7, 2019, https://www.ice.gov/doclib/facilityInspections/eloyDetCenterAZ_CL_02-07-2019.pdf.
6. Alisa Reznick, "Rep. Ansari Says ICE Refused Her Request to Speak with Constituents Detained in Eloy," KJZZ, July 23, 2025, https://www.kjzz.org/politics/2025-07-23/rep-ansari-says-ice-refused-her-request-to-speak-with-constituents-detained-in-eloy.
7. Yari M. Ansari, US House of Representatives, to Acting ICE Director Todd Lyons, September 4, 2025, https://ansari.house.gov/imo/media/doc/yari_letter_to_acting_director_todd_lyons.pdf.
8. Jonathan Blitzer, "The Congresswoman Criminalized for Visiting ICE Detainees," *New Yorker*, January 19, 2026, https://www.newyorker.com/magazine/2026/01/26/lamonica-mciver-congress-ice-jail-visit-felony-charges.
9. *Cruelty Campaign: Solitary Confinement in U.S. Immigration Detention* (Physicians for Human Rights, September 17, 2025), https://phr.org/our-work/resources/cruelty-campaign-solitary-confinement-in-u-s-immigration-detention/.
10. Oliver Peeples, "Dim Days, Bright Nights: A Hidden Cruelty of ICE Detention," *The Guardian*, October 20, 2025, https://www.theguardian.com/us-news/2025/oct/20/ice-facilities-lighting-overnight.
11. Martha von Werthern et al., "The Influence of Immigration Detention on Mental Health Outcomes: A Systematic Review," *BMC Psychiatry* 18, no. 382 (2018), https://doi.org/10.1186/s12888-018-1945-y.
12. *Immigration Enforcement: Actions Needed to Strengthen DHS Oversight of Conditions of Confinement and Reduce Risk of Deaths in Custody*, GAO-21-149 (Washington, DC: US

Government Accountability Office, 2021), https://www.gao.gov/products/gao-21-149.

13. *Thrive: A Blueprint for Policy and Public Officials for Self-Reliant Rural Communities Without Immigration Prisons* (Innovation Law Lab, June 2023), https://innovationlawlab.org/resource/thrive-blueprint-policy-and-public-officials-self-reliant-rural-communities-without.
14. Tom Meagher and Christie Thompson, "So You Think a New Prison Will Save Your Town?," *The Marshall Project*, June 14, 2016, https://www.themarshallproject.org/2016/06/14/so-you-think-a-new-prison-will-save-your-town.
15. Tracy Huling, "Building a Prison Economy in Rural America," in *Invisible Punishment: The Collateral Consequences of Mass Imprisonment*, ed. Marc Mauer and Meda Chesney-Lind (New York: New Press, 2002), https://www.prisonpolicy.org/scans/building.html.
16. Gregory Hooks et al., "Revisiting the Impact of Prison Building on Job Growth: Education, Incarceration, and County-Level Employment, 1976–2004," *Social Science Quarterly* 91, no. 1 (March 2010): 228–44, https://doi.org/10.1111/j.1540-6237.2010.00690.x.
17. "Officer Wellness and PTSD," One Voice United, accessed February 12, 2026, https://onevoiceunited.org/our-programs/officer-wellness-and-ptsd/; "Correctional Officer Wellness Project: Mental Health," One Voice United, September 2020, https://onevoiceunited.org/wp-content/uploads/2020/09/OneVoice_MentalHealth.pdf.
18. *Annual Report 2020: Reckoning with Justice* (Vera Institute of Justice, December 2020), https://www.vera.org/annual-report-2020-reckoning-with-justice.
19. John Washington, "ICE Mismanagement Created Coronavirus 'Hotbeds of Infection' in and Around Detention Centers," *The Intercept*, December 9, 2020, https://theintercept.

com/2020/12/09/ice-covid-detention-centers/.

20. Melissa del Bosque and Isabel Macdonald, "How Trump's Deportation Flights Are Putting Latin America and the Caribbean at Risk," *The Intercept*, June 26, 2020, https://theintercept.com/2020/06/26/coronavirus-ice-detention-deportation-haiti-guatemala/.
21. Joseph Nwadiuko et al., "Adult Hospitalizations from Immigration Detention in Louisiana and Texas, 2015–2018," *PLOS Global Public Health* 2, no. 8 (August 3, 2022): e0000432, https://doi.org/10.1371/journal.pgph.0000432.
22. Dhruv Mehrotra and Dell Cameron, "'They're Not Breathing': Inside the Chaos of ICE Detention Center 911 Calls," *Wired*, June 25, 2025, https://www.wired.com/story/ice-detention-center-911-emergencies/.
23. Yael Jácome, "The Effect of Immigration Enforcement on Crime Reporting: Evidence from Dallas," *Journal of Urban Economics* 128 (March 2022): 103395, https://doi.org/10.1016/j.jue.2021.103395.
24. Carolina Cuellar and John Washington, "As a Family Prepares to Self-Deport, a Tucson Group Helps Them Feel Less Alone," *Arizona Luminaria*, December 23, 2025, https://azluminaria.org/2025/12/23/tucson-immigrants-self-deportation-mental-health-support/.
25. Joanne Elgart Jennings, "ICE Detentions Bring Profits to Louisiana, but at What Cost?," *PBS NewsHour*, October 20, 2019, https://www.pbs.org/newshour/show/ice-detentions-bring-profits-to-louisiana-but-at-what-cost.
26. *Thrive: A Blueprint*.
27. Laurie Roberts, "CoreCivic Private Prisons Score Big While Arizona Schools Starve," *Arizona Republic*, January 10, 2022, https://www.azcentral.com/story/opinion/op-ed/laurieroberts/2022/01/10/corecivic-private-prisons-score-big-while-arizona-schools-starve/9159890002/.

3. "You Shall Do a Bad Job for the Germans"

1. "Ten Commandments of Noncooperation," available at https://ignitepeace.org/featured/ten-commandments-of-noncooperation/.
2. Sarah Sophie Flicker, "The Danes Resisted Fascism, and So Can We," *The Nation*, August 5, 2025, https://www.thenation.com/article/activism/danish-resistance/.
3. Michelle Castañeda, *Disappearing Rooms: The Hidden Theaters of Immigration Law* (Durham, NC: Duke University Press, 2023).
4. Castañeda, *Disappearing Rooms.*
5. Austin Kocher, "Data, Stories, and Justice: My Keynote Remarks at the Immigration Law & Justice of New York Gala," *Austin Kocher* (Substack newsletter), November 11, 2025, https://austinkocher.substack.com/p/data-stories-and-justice-my-keynote.
6. J. David McSwane and Hannah Allam, "Unfettered and Unaccountable: How Trump Is Building a Violent, Shadowy Federal Police Force," *ProPublica*, October 18, 2025, https://www.propublica.org/article/trump-dhs-ice-secret-police-civil-rights-unaccountable.
7. Carlos Ballesteros, "Illinois Legislature Passes Bill to Close State's Immigration Detention Centers," *Injustice Watch*, May 28, 2021, https://www.injusticewatch.org/civil-courts/immigration/2021/illinois-way-forward-immigration-detention-centers/.
8. "Victory! Private Prison Company Calls Off Plans for an Immigrant Detention Center in Elkhart County," ACLU of Indiana, January 26, 2018, https://www.aclu-in.org/news/victory-private-prison-company-calls-plans-immigrant-detention-center-elkhart-county/; Shayndi Raice, "Why One Trump County Rejected an Immigration-Detention Facility," *Wall Street Journal*, February 2, 2018, https://www.wsj.com/articles/why-one-trump-county-rejected-an-immigration-detention-facility-1517567401.

9. Shayndi Raice, "Why One Trump County Rejected an Immigration Detention Facility," *Wall Street Journal*, February 2, 2018, https://www.wsj.com/articles/why-one-trump-county-rejected-an-immigration-detention-facility-1517567401.
10. Dara Lind, "Immigration Prosecutors Were Told Not to Push for Deportation in Cases Like His. He Was Ordered Deported the Next Day," *ProPublica*, July 27, 2021, https://www.propublica.org/article/immigration-prosecutors-were-told-not-to-push-for-deportation-in-cases-like-his.
11. Silky Shah, *Unbuild Walls* (Chicago: Haymarket Books, 2024).
12. See Dean Spade, *Mutual Aid: Building Solidarity During This Crisis (and the Next)* (London: Verso, 2020).
13. Grant Mitchell, "Global Advocacy: Civil Society Engagement of Government on Alternatives to Immigration Detention," in *Challenging Immigration Detention: Academics, Activists and Policy-Makers*, ed. Michael J. Flynn and Matthew B. Flynn (Cheltenham, UK: Edward Elgar Publishing, 2017).
14. See Harsha Walia, *Border and Rule: Global Migration, Capitalism, and the Rise of Racist Nationalism* (Chicago: Haymarket Books, 2021).

4. ICE Power Map

1. Adam Cox, "Not So Exceptional: Adam Cox Exposes the Myth of 'Plenary Power' in Immigration Law," interview, NYU School of Law, March 13, 2025, https://www.law.nyu.edu/news/ideas/adam-cox-immigration-exceptionalism-plenary-power.
2. See Harsha Walia, *Border and Rule: Global Migration, Capitalism, and the Rise of Racist Nationalism* (Chicago: Haymarket Books, 2021).
3. Rebecca Cassler, "BIA Ruling Strips Immigration Judges of Bond Authority, All but Guaranteeing Mandatory Detention for Undocumented Immigrants," American Immigration Council, September 12, 2025, https://www.americanim-

migrationcouncil.org/blog/bia-ruling-immigration-judges-bond-mandatory-detention-undocumented-immigrants/.

4. American Civil Liberties Union, "New ACLU Report Reveals How the Trump Administration Is Using Local Police to Build a National Deportation-Policing Force Through the 287(g) Program," press release, February 26, 2026, https://www.aclu.org/press-releases/new-aclu-report-reveals-how-the-trump-administration-is-using-local-police-to-build-a-national-deportation-policing-force-through-the-287g-program.
5. Donald J. Trump (@realDonaldTrump), "I am pleased announce that the Former ICE Director, and stalwart on Border Control, Tom Homan, will be joining the Trump Administration," November 10, 2024, https://truthsocial.com/@realDonaldTrump/posts/113462412414821782.
6. "ICE Announces Historic 120% Manpower Increase, Thanks to Recruitment Campaign That Brought in 12,000 Officers and Agents," US Immigration and Customs Enforcement news release, January 3, 2026, https://www.dhs.gov/news/2026/01/03/ice-announces-historic-120-manpower-increase-thanks-recruitment-campaign-brought.
7. Eric Westervelt et al., "Mapping ICE's Expanding Footprint, and the Communities Fighting Back," NPR, March 23, 2026, https://www.npr.org/2026/03/23/g-s1-114107/ices-growing-detention-footprint-and-the-communities-fighting-back; *Immigration Detention Expansion in Trump's Second Term* (American Immigration Council, January 2026), https://www.americanimmigrationcouncil.org/wp-content/uploads/2026/01/immigration-detention-report.pdf.
8. "Guaranteed Minimums in Detention Contracts," Detention Watch Network, https://www.detentionwatchnetwork.org/sites/default/files/Guaranteed%20Minimums%20in%20Detention%20Contracts.pdf.

9. Alina Das, "The Law and Lawlessness of U.S. Immigration Detention," *Harvard Law Review* 138, no. 5 (March 2025): 1186–1259, https://harvardlawreview.org/print/vol-138/the-law-and-lawlessness-of-u-s-immigration-detention/.
10. Das, "Law and Lawlessness."
11. Gillian E. Metzger, "The Constitutional Duty to Supervise," *Yale Law Journal* 124, no. 5 (2015): 1836–1933, https://yalelawjournal.org/pdf/a.1836.Metzger.1933_wd4sdxbs.pdf.
12. Adam Isacson et al., "Denouncing Into the Void: The Dismantling of Internal Oversight and Accountability at DHS," Washington Office on Latin America and Kino Border Initiative, March 19, 2026, https://www.wola.org/analysis/denouncing-into-the-void-the-dismantling-of-internal-oversight-and-accountability-at-dhs/.
13. Isabel Del Mastro et al., "ICE Inspections Plummeted as Detentions Soared in 2025," Project On Government Oversight, October 15, 2025, https://www.pogo.org/investigates/ice-inspections-plummeted-as-detentions-soared-in-2025.
14. Richard A. Webster and Bobbi-Jeanne Misick, "Louisiana's Parole System Pushed Immigrants Toward Deportation in 'Operation Geaux,'" *ProPublica*, December 8, 2025, https://www.propublica.org/article/louisiana-parole-deportation-jeff-landry-operation-geaux.
15. Cassandra Stephenson, "West Tennessee Town Approves CoreCivic to Run Immigration Detention Facility After Chaotic Meeting," *Tennessee Lookout*, August 13, 2025, https://tennesseelookout.com/2025/08/13/west-tenn-town-approves-corecivic-to-run-immigration-detention-facility-after-chaotic-meeting/.
16. Cassandra Stephenson, "Mason Leaders Approve ICE Facility After Chaotic Meeting," *Memphis Flyer*, August 13, 2025, https://memphis-flyer.com/mason-leaders-approve-ice-facility-after-chaotic-meeting.

17. Matt Scott, "Atlanta Police Searched License Plate Reader Network for Immigrants, Records Show," Atlanta Community Press Collective, November 13, 2025, https://atlpresscollective.com/2025/11/13/atlanta-police-flock-immigration-searches/.
18. "Immigration Detention Statistics: A Retrospective and a Look Forward," Transactional Records Access Clearinghouse, Syracuse University, January 2025, https://tracreports.org/reports/753/.
19. Wendy Sawyer and Peter Wagner, "Only 8% of Confined People Are Held in Private Prisons," graph, Prison Policy Initiative, 2025, https://www.prisonpolicy.org/graphs/pie2025_private_facilities.html.
20. Nancy Hiemstra and Deirdre Conlon, *Immigration Detention Inc.: The Big Business of Locking up Migrants* (London: Pluto Press, 2025).
21. "Q2 2025 Earnings Conference Call" (transcript), GEO Group, August 6, 2025, https://seekingalpha.com/article/4809792-the-geo-group-inc-geo-q2-2025-earnings-call-transcript.
22. Laura Romero et al., "Private Prison Firm CoreCivic Gave $500K to Trump's Inauguration, Highlighting Industry's Support," ABC News, January 29, 2025, https://abcnews.com/US/private-prison-firm-corecivic-gave-500k-trumps-inauguration/story?id=118218707.
23. "The GEO Group Awarded Contract by U.S. Immigration and Customs Enforcement for Provision of Skip Tracing Services," GEO Group news release, December 22, 2025, https://investors.geogroup.com/news-releases/news-release-details/geo-group-awarded-contract-us-immigration-and-customs-1.
24. Thomas Ferraro, "Raising a $1-a-Day Wage Seems Like a No-Brainer. Not to Congress," *In These Times*, July 21, 2022, https://inthesetimes.com/article/dollar-a-day-wages-immi-

gration-detention-geo-corecivic-congress.

25. Nwauzor v. The GEO Group, Inc., 21-36024 (9th Cir. 2025).
26. Brief for the United States as Amicus Curiae in Support of Appellant, Nwauzor v. The GEO Group, Inc., Nos. 21-36024, 21-36025 (9th Cir. Feb. 21, 2024), https://assets.law360news.com/1806000/1806150/amicus%20brief.pdf.
27. *The Infiltrators*, directed by Alex Rivera and Cristina Ibarra (2019).
28. Graham v. Connor, 490 U.S. 386 (1989).
29. Noem v. Vasquez Perdomo, 606 U.S. (2025).

5. A Prison Town Says No

1. Sherman Smith, "ICE Rushed No-Bid Contract to Pay CoreCivic $4.2M per Month to Hold Immigrants at Kansas Prison," *Kansas Reflector*, July 1, 2025, https://kansasreflector.com/2025/07/01/ice-rushed-no-bid-contract-to-pay-corecivic-4-2m-per-month-to-hold-immigrants-at-kansas-prison/.
2. Cary Aspinwall, "Why a Prison Town That Voted for Trump Is Fighting an Immigration Detention Facility," *The Marshall Project*, July 1, 2025, https://www.themarshallproject.org/2025/07/01/leavenworth-kansas-immigration-prison-fight.
3. Casey Tolan, "Biden Vowed to Close Federal Private Prisons, but Prison Companies Are Finding Loopholes to Keep Them Open," CNN, November 12, 2021, https://www.cnn.com/2021/11/12/politics/biden-private-prisons-immigration-detention-centers-invs.
4. City of Leavenworth v. CoreCivic, Inc., No. LV-2025-CV-000180, Petition (Dist. Ct. Leavenworth Cnty., Kan., filed May 23, 2025), https://mediaassets.kshb.com/NWT/Sam/LV-2025-CV-000180%20-%20Petition..pdf.
5. Morgan Chilson, "Leavenworth Wins Temporary Restraining Order Barring CoreCivic from Taking ICE Detainees,"

Kansas Reflector, June 4, 2025, https://kansasreflector.com/2025/06/04/leavenworth-wins-restraining-order-barring-corecivic-from-taking-ice-detainees/.

6. Emma Murphy, "Oklahomans Denounce Potential ICE Processing Center at OKC City Council Meeting," *Oklahoma Voice*, January 27, 2026, https://oklahomavoice.com/2026/01/27/oklahomans-denounce-potential-ice-processing-center-at-okc-city-council-meeting/; Derrick James, "City of Durant, Choctaw Nation Take Action against Rumored ICE Facility," *NonDoc*, January 14, 2026, https://nondoc.com/2026/01/14/city-of-durant-choctaw-nation-take-action-against-rumored-ice-facility/; Celisa Calacal, "Kansas City Agency Cuts Ties with Company Selling Warehouse for ICE Detention Center," KCUR, February 9, 2026, https://www.kcur.org/politics-elections-and-government/2026-02-09/kansas-city-agency-cuts-ties-with-company-selling-warehouse-for-ice-detention-center.
7. *Management Alert—Immediate Removal of All Detainees from the Torrance County Detention Facility*, OIG-22-31 (US Department of Homeland Security, Office of Inspector General, March 16, 2022), https://www.oig.dhs.gov/reports/2022/management-alert-immediate-removal-all-detainees-torrance-county-detention-facility/oig-22-31-mar22-mgmtalert.
8. Austin Fisher, "Sewage Flooding Cells Inside Torrance County ICE Prison Again, Advocates Say," *Source New Mexico*, May 2, 2025, https://sourcenm.com/2025/05/02/sewage-flooding-cells-inside-torrance-county-ice-prison-again-advocates-say/.
9. Manisha Sinha, *The Slave's Cause: A History of Abolition* (New Haven: Yale University Press, 2016).
10. Adrianna Torres-García and Jasmine Rivera, "A Victory for Abolitionists: ICE-Run Immigration Prison Shuts Down Today," *Truthout*, January 31, 2023, https://truthout.org/

articles/a-victory-for-abolitionists-ice-run-immigration-prison-shuts-down-today/.

11. "Make the Road v. Leinbach," Free Migration Project, n.d., https://freemigrationproject.org/make-the-road-v-leinbach/.
12. Debbie Wasserman Schultz to Jeff Nelson, October 13, 2021, https://www.documentcloud.org/documents/265196-debbie-wasserman-schultz-letter-to-jeff-nelson.html.
13. Susannah Bryan, "Town Blames Rival for Blocking Big-Money Detention Center. Now It Wants $150 Million," *South Florida Sun Sentinel*, October 12, 2021, https://www.sun-sentinel.com/2021/10/12/town-blames-rival-for-blocking-big-money-detention-center-now-it-wants-150-million/.
14. Julie Steinberg, "Private Immigrant Detention Center Expansion Restriction Stands," *Bloomberg Law*, November 14, 2019, https://news.bloomberglaw.com/white-collar-and-criminal-law/private-immigrant-detention-center-expansion-restriction-stands.
15. Lillian Reed, "Howard County Revokes Permit for ICE Detention Facility in Elkridge," *Baltimore Banner*, February 2, 2026, https://www.thebanner.com/politics-power/national-politics/ice-building-elkridge-maryland-EC6OBV7IZFB57A4UUPWZULUN7Y/.
16. Claudia Valenzuela et al., *Lives in Peril: How Ineffective Inspections Make ICE Complicit in Detention Center Abuse* (National Immigrant Justice Center; Detention Watch Network, October 2015), https://immigrantjustice.org/research/lives-in-peril-how-ineffective-inspections-make-ice-complicit-in-detention-center-abuse/.

6. Creative Resistance

1. Aisha Wallace-Palomares, "The First National Website Dedicated to Documenting ICE License Plates Is Here," *LA Taco*, December 23, 2025, https://lataco.com/ice-license-plate-tracker.

2. Dan Stockman, "Sisters of Social Service Ends Leasing Contract with Enterprise over ICE Connection," *National Catholic Reporter*, October 23, 2025, https://www.ncronline.org/sisters-social-service-ends-leasing-contract-enterprise-over-ice-connection.
3. Associated Press, "Federal Prosecutors Charge 3 Activists with 'Doxing' of ICE Agent in Los Angeles," *PBS NewsHour*, September 29, 2025, https://www.pbs.org/newshour/nation/federal-prosecutors-charge-3-activists-with-doxing-of-ice-agent-in-los-angeles.
4. Rey Wences, Gabe Gonzalez, and Joselyn Walsh, "How We've Resisted ICE: Street Lessons from Chicago," interview by Kelly Hayes, *Movement Memos* (podcast), *Truthout*, December 11, 2025, https://truthout.org/audio/how-weve-resisted-ice-street-lessons-from-chicago/.
5. Associated Press, "Texts Appear to Show Border Patrol Agent Bragging About Shooting a Woman in Chicago," WTOP News, November 6, 2025, https://wtop.com/national/2025/11/texts-appear-to-show-border-patrol-agent-bragging-about-shooting-a-woman-in-chicago/.
6. Robert Mackey, "Border Patrol Chief Praised Federal Agent Who Shot US Citizen in Chicago," *The Guardian*, February 11, 2026, https://www.theguardian.com/us-news/2026/feb/11/gregory-bovino-praised-agent-shot-us-citizen-chicago.
7. Bill Gallegos, "How LA Defeated Donald Trump," *The Nation*, December 16, 2025, https://www.thenation.com/article/society/how-la-defeated-donald-trump/.
8. Chicago Teachers Union Local 1 (@ctulocal1), "As a history teacher, CTU President Davis Gates knows that Chicago's past shows us the way forward," Instagram, October 16, 2025, https://www.instagram.com/reel/DP5Ir5sAFs1/.

Conclusion: Risking Our Necks

1. Jesus Rodríguez Martinez, Northwest Detention Center, Washington, 2023. Grace Deng, "Immigrant Detainees Resort to Hunger Strikes in Protest of Conditions at Tacoma Facility," *Washington State Standard*, November 17, 2023, https://washingtonstatestandard.com/2023/11/17/immigrant-detainees-resort-to-hunger-strikes-in-protest-of-conditions-at-tacoma-facility/.
2. Unnamed men, Krome Service Processing Center, Florida, 2025. Claire Healy and Syra Ortiz-Blanes, "Cuba Detainees Launch Protest at Krome Detention Center, Line Up to Form SOS Signs," *Miami Herald*, June 5, 2025, https://www.miamiherald.com/news/local/immigration/article307951115.html.
3. Unnamed man, Otay Mesa Detention Center, California, 2026. Aisha Wallace-Polomares, "Exclusive: Detention Center Captives Are Throwing Lotion Bottles Wrapped with Notes to Organizers Outside Otay Mesa Facility," *LA Taco*, February 5, 2026, https://lataco.com/captive-lotion-bottle-note?utm_source=substack&utm_medium=email.
4. Yana Kunichoff and John Washington, "Possible Immigration Detention Center at Former Marana Prison Draws Community Outcry," *Arizona Luminaria*, October 27, 2025, https://azluminaria.org/2025/10/27/possible-immigration-detention-center-at-former-marana-prison-draws-community-outcry/.
5. "Crowd Control, Appeasement, Vanguardism, and the General Strike: An Analysis from the Twin Cities," CrimethInc., February 1, 2026, https://crimethinc.com/2026/02/01/crowd-control-appeasement-vanguardism-and-the-general-strike-an-analysis-from-the-twin-cities.
6. Stewart Huntington, "'Full Circle': AIM Patrols Back on Minneapolis Streets as Tensions Rise," *ICT News*, January 18, 2026, https://ictnews.org/news/full-circle-aim-patrols-back-

on-minneapolis-streets-as-tensions-rise.

7. David Graeber, "The Shock of Victory," *Rolling Thunder: An Anarchist Journal of Dangerous Living*, no. 5 (2007), available at The Anarchist Library, https://theanarchistlibrary.org/library/david-graeber-the-shock-of-victory.
8. Graeber, "The Shock of Victory."
9. Graeber, "The Shock of Victory."
10. Rümeysa Öztürk, "Op-Ed: 'Even God Cannot Hear Us Here': What I Witnessed Inside an ICE Women's Prison," *Tufts Daily*, July 17, 2025, https://www.tuftsdaily.com/article/2025/07/op-ed-even-god-cannot-hear-us-here-what-i-witnessed-inside-an-ice-womens-prison.
11. Reyyan Bilge, "I've Known Rümeysa Öztürk for More Than a Decade. Her Detention Is a Betrayal of American Values," *Boston Globe*, April 2, 2025, https://www.bostonglobe.com/2025/04/02/opinion/tufts-grad-student-detained-rumeysa-ozturk/.
12. Öztürk, "Even God Cannot Hear Us Here."
13. Hannah Allam, "American Rendition: Rümeysa Öztürk's Journey from Ph.D. Scholar to Trump Target Languishing in Louisiana Cell," *ProPublica*, April 13, 2025, https://www.propublica.org/article/rumeysa-ozturk-best-friend-inside-story-tufts-trump-louisiana-ice.
14. Öztürk, "Even God Cannot Hear Us Here."
15. Öztürk, "Even God Cannot Hear Us Here."

INDEX

ABOUT HAYMARKET BOOKS

Haymarket Books is a radical, independent, nonprofit book publisher based in Chicago. Our mission is to publish books that contribute to struggles for social and economic justice. We strive to make our books a vibrant and organic part of social movements and the education and development of a critical, engaged, and internationalist left.

We take inspiration and courage from our namesakes, the Haymarket Martyrs, who gave their lives fighting for a better world. Their 1886 struggle for the eight-hour day—which gave us May Day, the international workers' holiday—reminds workers around the world that ordinary people can organize and struggle for their own liberation. These struggles—against oppression, exploitation, environmental devastation, and war—continue today across the globe.

Since our founding in 2001, Haymarket has published more than nine hundred titles. Radically independent, we seek to drive a wedge into the risk-averse world of corporate book publishing. Our authors include Angela Y. Davis, Arundhati Roy, Keeanga-Yamahtta Taylor, Eve Ewing, Aja Monet, Mariame Kaba, Naomi Klein, Rebecca Solnit, Mohammed El-Kurd, José Olivarez, Noam Chomsky, Winona LaDuke, Robyn Maynard, Leanne Betasamosake Simpson, Howard Zinn, Mike Davis, Marc Lamont Hill, Dave Zirin, Astra Taylor, and Amy Goodman, among many other leading writers of our time. We are also the trade publishers of the acclaimed Historical Materialism Book Series.

Haymarket also manages a vibrant community organizing and event space in Chicago, Haymarket House, the popular Haymarket Books Live event series and podcast, and the annual Socialism Conference.

ABOUT THE AUTHOR

© Aaron Schasse

John Washington has written for *The New York Review of Books*, *The Washington Post*, *The Nation*, and *The Intercept*, among other outlets. He is the author of *The Case for Open Borders* and *The Dispossessed: A Story of Asylum at the US-Mexican Border and Beyond* and a translator of books by Anabel Hernández, Sandra Rodríguez Nieto, and Óscar Martínez and Juan José Martínez. He lives in Tucson, Arizona, where he is a staff writer for *Lookout*.